Más Que Vencedores

A Story of Miracles

By

Deb Coutts
and
Annette Vickers

www.xulonpress.com

This book is
dedicated to the Glory of God.

Proceeds go to

Más Que Vencedores
a Sports' Church and ministry
located in
Santa Ana, El Salvador

MAC Sports
Ministerio Atletico Cristiano
based in Managua, Nicaragua

and
PAN Missions
a ministry to the poor of Nicaragua
based in Guelph, Ontario, Canada
with local headquarters in Managua, Nicaragua

TABLE OF CONTENTS

Introduction xi

The Beginning 19

The Call to Work with Young People.........27

Oscar 37

José 47

Mariceli...57

Nena 65

Gerardo 73

David Alexander 81

Miriam 91

Omar..99

Yolanda 109

Ena 119

Brenda..127

Betty 137

The Two Rubis 147

Carlos...161

Codicil to Carlos' Story............................175

Ceci...179

Yanira...187

Reyna..197

Lily..211

Angels and Revelations.............................225

Prophecies by Lily....................................243

God Looks After Us..................................251

Parting Words from Melvin......................257

A Final Word...261

Pastor Melvin Vásquez

With Love

Melvin Vásquez
El Salvador

INTRODUCTION

Give ear to my words, O Lord, consider my sighing.

Listen to my cry for help, my King and my God, for to

you I pray. Morning by morning O Lord, you hear my

voice; morning by morning I lay my requests before

you and wait in expectation.

Psalm 5:1-3

I feel as if we have stumbled upon our own little treasure trove! I had read a little about healings and miraculous events taking place in the United States and in other places around the world, but here we were, encountering the supernatural for ourselves. And, it all happened acciden-tally…or is that providentially?

Deb Coutts and I were leading a small PAN Mission team doing some projects in and around our base in Managua, Nicaragua. The focus of this group had changed from its inception and we decided at the last minute to end the visit by taking a trip up to Santa Ana in El Salvador. While there, we planned to join up with a Sports' Team from Tyndale University in Toronto that was doing a three week outreach program led by our friend, Pastor Melvin Vásquez. When we arrived in Santa Ana about 8:00p.m. we pulled up in front of Más Que Vencedores (More Than Conquerors) church anticipating that we would be taken right to our billets. However, there was a service in progress and we were invited in to be introduced. We dutifully stumbled in and shook a few hands, but after a fourteen hour van ride no one was in the mood to stay. We found out later that it was a pity we didn't. We would have witnessed God at work!

I had met Pastor Melvin the year previously on a visit to Santa Ana when he was giving us some leadership training for our fledgling new ministry, MAC Sports. At that time I overheard Melvin talking on the phone and knew from his joyful reaction that he had just received good news. He told me later it was about a lady they had been praying for named Miriam, and that she had just received a healing from God. But, the amazing part of the story was that God had removed a cancerous tumour from her stomach through "heavenly surgery" while she lay in her bed. The Lord left a visible scar on her belly as proof that He had been at work. That story stayed in my mind for over a year and I determined that when I returned to El Salvador, I wanted to go and visit this lady personally. Now here we were, and my opportunity was at hand.

Melvin kindly set up an appointment with Miriam, and Deb along with a couple of others from our team, decided to join us. However, while we were having a coffee together just before the visit, Melvin casually mentioned that Miriam's was not the only healing that had taken place. We pressed him to explain further and he gave us lots more examples of miraculous healings.

After our visit with Miriam, Deb and I urged Melvin to try to set up more appointments for us. He was as good as his word, and the next day we spent several hours visiting various families to learn about what God had done for them. After a while, our heads were spinning and we needed to take time to process the incredible stories we had just heard. Besides, Melvin had to get back to hosting his Tyndale University team!

At first we were just going to use these stories in the "PAN Press", our Mission newsletter and also post them on our website. But, after thinking it over, Deb and I decided that if Melvin concurred, we would collate all the stories in book form. Melvin liked the idea and so the project got underway. There were still lots more individuals and families to interview so it was determined that I would return to El Salvador a few weeks later.

On that next trip, I was able to spend more time visiting around with Melvin. We were welcomed into each home and all those interviewed shared enthusiastically about what God had done for them. Occasionally other family members would chime in or nod in agreement as the stories unfolded. It was heart-warming and very moving to sit as a guest in humble surroundings and gaze into the faces of these wonderful people. As they re-lived their encounter with God, their emotions would sometimes take over and several tears were shed. At the end, we hugged and prayed and gave thanks to God for his goodness.

Some of the healings happened instantaneously but most of them did not take place suddenly in a long healing line in front of the altar. Although there was a defining moment when the recipient knew that healing had occurred, the whole thing was usually a process. A lot of prayer, both individual and corporate, preceded the event. The prayer chain, called La Peña, (composed of the majority of the congregation) was instrumental in practically all of the miracles. This group prays faithfully every morning at 3:00a.m., each one in their own home.

In our chats with various people, we also learned about other supernatural occurrences....angels, columns of fire, heavenly anointings of oil. But nobody boasted about their experiences because the events themselves were very personal to the people involved. Without exception, each experience had a profound influence on the recipient.

Another important point is that many of the healings can be verified by local doctors, and we saw several x-rays and medical reports ourselves. Also, family members, neighbours, friends and church members all gave testimonies to the healings.

To me, the church Más Que Vencedores, epitomizes what I think a New Testament church should be. There is genuine love and concern for one another. Although most of the parishioners are poor they donate food every week for families poorer than they are. Their focus is outreach, and everyone is involved. Sports is their biggest venue for winning young people to Christ but they are developing more strategies to win the lost. Sharing the gospel is the priority and signs and wonders just seem to follow naturally.

As well as learning more about the miracles in Más Que Vencedores church, I learned a lot more about Pastor Melvin. He has an amazing testimony which he shares in this book. This man is 100% devoted to God. His enthusiasm for the Lord is contagious and he is a joy to be around. God is doing wonderful things through his ministry, and if the prophetic words about him prove accurate, there are lots more amazing things still to come.

It is our hope that these stories, told right from the mouths of the individuals involved, will bring you renewed hope and encouragement, and reignite that spark that will set you on fire once more and rekindle your passion for God.

Blessings,

Annette Vickers

PAN Missions

THE BEGINNING
By Pastor Melvin Vásquez

In the last days, God says, I will pour out my Spirit on all people. Your sons and daughters will prophesy, your young men will see visions, your old men will dream dreams. Even on my servants, both men and women, I will pour out my Spirit in those days, and they will prophesy.

Acts 2:17-18

I received Jesus Christ as my personal Saviour at the age of twelve, was baptized at the age of thirteen and received the baptism of the Holy Spirit this same year, 1980. I remember these experiences as if they were yesterday.

The succeeding years were wonderful enjoying the presence of God. The Lord guided me into serving Him in various ways and blessed me richly. I was especially active in working with teenagers and with young children in the schools. Little by little I became a leader in these areas and I served with enthusiasm. In time, God moved me into specific projects that sometimes seemed difficult and incomprehensible, but in the end always resulted in a great blessing.

Then, I met a pretty girl named Dina who captured my heart, and we were married in 1988. One year later, our first child, Karen, was born. But, bit by bit, there was a subtle change in me. I no longer had my parents guiding me in my decision making. I started to feel like a big man in control of my own life. My decisions were not always wise ones.

Then something unexpected happened. The company I worked for decided to transfer me to the capital, San Salvador, and this change drastically impacted my life. I was confronted with a direction that was totally foreign to me.

Now I could see my family only on weekends and there was no more church, no more serving God. My life in ministry began to tumble and finally ceased altogether. My personal relationship with Jesus grew weaker day by day until I realized I had lost His presence within me.

Eventually I returned to Santa Ana and I tried to get re-established in the church but it was very difficult. A new burden had its hold on me—alcoholism. I fought to rid myself of this big problem but all my struggle was in vain. Dina and my daughter would go off to church on Sunday morning but I would stay at home. I would cry out to God and ask Him to forgive me, but on Monday evening after work I would be right back in the bars. Then one day it was as if God was saying, "Enough! Time's up!" It was about two o'clock in the morning and I was just returning home after a long night partying with my friends, actually the third night in a row of drinking and staying out till the wee small hours. I remember I was travelling on a lonely road home

21

going about 100 kilometres per hour. Then, while rounding a bend in the road, I remember closing my eyes for just a moment. When I opened them, a large stationary tractor trailer was right in front of me! My car slammed into the back of the parked trailer at full speed and the impact totally destroyed my vehicle. The front of the car was smashed in like a pop can. The steering wheel struck my head as it was pushed upwards.

I was trapped with two broken legs, a broken arm and my head split in two! Incredibly I was still alive but there was no one around to help. It's different in El Salvador than it is in Canada and the United States. In the middle of the night, people stay home because it's not considered safe to be out on the roads. So there I was, utterly alone. This was between God and me!

In the space of just a few minutes, I lost a lot of blood. Part of my face was not in its proper place, my head was split open into two halves from my nose to the back of the crown, and my left eye was dangling out of its socket. But I remained conscious and looked around the vehicle. I touched my body and felt the blood running down my face, and right then I made a decision to talk to God. I began by placing each member of my family into His hands, asking Him to take care of them. I pleaded for my wife and daughter and for my mother until I started to tremble and go into shock because of the loss of blood. And in this moment, when I felt that my life was escaping me, I asked the Lord to forgive me. I remember my words were something like: "Receive me Lord, I beg you. Forgive my wicked ways."

My eyes were closing and I was ready to give up my spirit to the Lord when I heard a loud cry: "Melvin!!!"

What had happened? It was the owner of the tractor trailer. At 2:00a.m. he was tossing and turning in his bed unable to sleep. He suddenly felt the necessity to go out in the early hours of the morning to check on the security of his vehicle! Incredibly, this man was actually someone who knew me!

The area of the crash was quite a bit outside of the city and practically nobody passed this way, especially in the middle of the night. But I have no doubt that this was all under God's control. It was all part of His rescue plan. To me, it wasn't actually my friend calling my name, it was the Lord.

I don't know how he managed it, but my friend was able to get me out of the car and took me to the nearest hospital.

Later as I was lying on a hospital bed I asked myself, "Why am I still alive?" Then I realized I was in the operating room and there were all kinds of doctors around me having an earnest discussion. I could hear everything that the doctors were saying about me. They said I would lose my left eye, that they didn't know the total effects from the severe head injury, and that they might as well just stitch me up. I learned later that I underwent three hours of surgery.

The following morning, my wife Dina arrived at the hospital and paced uneasily around the ward which had several beds. I was so swollen and unrecognizable that Dina didn't know which patient was me. Finally, one of the nurses took her by the arm and guided her to the foot of my bed and said to her, "This is your husband." My head was the colour purple and the size of a basketball. I wanted to call out to her, "Sweetheart, it's me. I'm alive and I love you". But I couldn't say a word. My teeth had been pushed up into the roof of my mouth and everything was now sewn shut. Dina's reaction was to collapse on the floor.

Eventually my wife sat down by the side of my bed. I remember there was a tiny little opening in my injured left eye, and from this came tears that dropped on to Dina's hand. It was my way of saying to her, "Please forgive me."

People who saw the smashed up car said that there was no way anyone could have survived. But I did! Each day of my recuperation I would ask God, "Why have you spared my life?" It appeared that God had big plans for me, and this was just the beginning of a life full of miracles.

THE CALL TO WORK WITH YOUNG PEOPLE

By Pastor Melvin Vásquez

I raised you up for this very purpose,

that I might display my power in you and that my name

might be proclaimed in all the earth.

Romans 9:15b

After months and months of rehabilitation, I found myself at a new stage in my life with God, and He was able to continue His purpose through me. When I saw young people hanging out on the street corners, smoking and drinking and generally disparaging one another, I looked at them through new eyes. I realized there was little difference between them and me. Now, they were important to me. Now there was a real necessity for me to help these young people.

I soon realized that the time I spent experimenting with alcohol, away from God, still had a great purpose. All things work together for good to those that love God! Previously, I had preached to young people to quit the habits that were ruining their lives. Now I preached that all human efforts are in vain, and that to be set free from a destructive habit would require the power of God. He alone is able to break the powers of addiction. I am able to preach with authority since I have learned to live out the Word of God and because I have seen the fruits and results of His power in me.

At one time I had been a professional soccer player but after the accident I couldn't play any more. However, I still loved the sport and God told me I was now going to use my acquired skills to reach out to young people. It all began

when I was standing out on a street corner near my home

listening to Christian worship songs being sung in a nearby

house. Some adults were having a nice worship time but their

teenage children were hanging out on the streets in gangs,

smoking, swearing and drinking. "You are going to work

with these kids" God told me. So, I picked out ten of the

worst and wrote their names down on a list. Then I tacked it

to the wall beside our dining room table. When I said grace

before each meal, I prayed for these ten young men at the

same time. That continued for two months, then it was time

for action! I invited these ten young men to come and have a

meeting at my house on a particular evening. Incredibly, all

ten showed up.

That first meeting, I shared values and biblical principles

in a non-threatening manner. We didn't even use a Bible,

except to mention it as being God's word. We didn't sing any

Christian songs. But I did teach them to pray. They learned that praying is just having a conversation with God. The second week, all of them came back to the next meeting saying that they had really enjoyed what they had heard the week previously, and many of them brought along some friends. That night we had twenty-five young people at the meeting. I had to look for a room to rent big enough to hold everyone. Week after week, more and more young people came until close to eighty of them started showing up every week! We split up into five groups to accommodate everyone.

Now we were ready to pass into the second phase. We started a soccer league and within three months we had formed ten teams. In six months that grew to sixteen teams and in nine months we had twenty-four teams. Today, we have over five hundred young people playing in soccer leagues. We have also just recently started a league for girls and this year we will begin a soccer school for younger children. At every game and activity we talk about God, share testimonies and pray together. This is having a great impact on these young lives. We are able to chat about their personal needs and their problems and show these kids that the Bible offers them a hope that they never realized existed!

Many of the young people started receiving Christ and the group of volunteers grew, but, we had a little problem. The church that I attended did not like the method we were using and declined to offer us any help. We had lots of new converts but no place to send them to be discipled. At that point we were reaching about three hundred young people with the gospel but we had no church where we could all meet together. The only thing we could do was send them to the church closest to where they lived. It was hard not being able to do adequate follow-up ,but we didn't doubt that God was working because lots of the youth were serving in the churches around the city and bearing much fruit for the kingdom of God.

The Decision to Found a Church

I did not really understand how it was possible that a strategy that was bringing young people to the feet of Jesus Christ would not be accepted by my pastor. Then one day the volunteers asked me if we could have a meeting and a Bible study just for them. I remember that about fifteen people came to that first meeting in one of the homes. We really felt that God was with us so we decided to meet every Wednesday to do a Bible Study. But little by little it changed to become a service of worship. The number of leaders grew and we had to rent places big enough to hold us all. We grew to twenty-five then forty people and we had to keep renting bigger places. This was a crucial turning point. Our group set a date for a special meeting and that night they all sat around me and said, "Melvin, this is the time to put aside the sports for a moment. We are all in agreement that it's time to start a new church and we want you to be the pastor!"

I couldn't sleep that night. My head was spinning. I had never dreamed of starting up a church, and even less of being its pastor! I spoke with my own pastor and he heartily gave me the endorsement to initiate a new work. And so began our church, Más Que Vencedores—More Than Conquerors.

In six more months we were one hundred people strong and we had to find yet another place to meet. So we chose a bigger location, large enough to hold two hundred and fifty people. This is our current building. Now, ten months have passed since our inception and we have a congregation of more than one hundred and seventy. My petition to God is to end this year with two hundred people and day by day He is adding to our numbers.

La Peña

One time, one of the young people from our church became ill and had to be admitted to hospital. He had a serious liver condition and surgery was done. However, he ran into complications and his condition became grave. The doctors were not sure that he would survive. I went to see him and he told me that he had spent an unusual time talking with God in the middle of the night. He woke up at precisely 3:00 in the morning and started having a very special chat with God. He felt that at that time in the morning it was as if the heavens had opened up and God was hanging on his every word. He asked me to join him in praying at the same time the following morning, so at 3:00a.m. we communicated by telephone, then hung up and prayed, knowing that we were each at our personal altar united in prayer. This continued for a week and my young friend got better and better. On the following Monday I was about to go and visit him again at the hospital when he called me to tell me that I should visit him in his house because he was doing so well that they had sent him home!

This prayer time had been so spectacular that I decided to share this idea with the rest of the church. Not everyone was as excited about it as I was but twenty hands went up in the service to say that they would join me in early-morning prayer. About a month later, our first miracle happened. Then before we knew it we had a network of one hundred people praying at 3:00a.m., communicating first with a partner, and then going into prayer. We made a list of twenty petitions together to pray over and decided to additionally meet on Monday nights to pray through that list in one large group. The petitions dealt with a variety of illnesses....AIDS, tumours, infections...as well as problems at home, economic troubles, the need for employment, and much more. Our network was called La Peña—The Fan Club, that is, God's Fan Club!

The Time of the Miracles

One month after starting La Peña, God began to answer our petitions. From one Monday to the next, people were testifying about the miracles God had done in their lives. The next thing we decided was to have Prayer Vigils, praying as a congregation from 5:00p.m. to 1:30a.m. God manifested Himself every time on these special occasions, and each time, the manifestations were stronger. Soon we were receiving news of cancers disappearing, children being restored to health, healing from HIV, visible operations by the hand of God, and many more stories that you will read about in this book.

OSCAR

*W*hen I first met Oscar Gutierrez, I thought of him as a timid young man who was very reserved. But little by little he connected with the young people of our church. Oscar lives in a simple house in a very poor barrio with his mother and brother. He is a faithful church attendee when his work schedule permits, but he has a constant relationship with the Lord. He is single and waiting on God to bring the right woman into his life. We are sure that God is preparing her even now.

Oscar has become very dear to us all. In some ways he is like a child and in other ways like a man. But that just makes it easy for him to relate to the teenagers as well as the older people in our church. He is fascinated by "transformer toys" and can sit and manipulate them for a long time. He also loves bike riding. I remember that before Oscar knew he was healed, he joined us on a long, long bike ride to Lake Coatepeque. Although we biked for kilometres he was able to keep up. We fished and swam and then did the long trek home. Oscar was with us as "one of the boys".

After attending *Más Que Vencedores* church for a while, Oscar decided to be baptized. He was a part of the very first group of baptismal candidates that we had in the church. He, along with the others, took the three month preparation course then on a Sunday morning we all headed out to Lake Coatepeque.

I was in the water receiving each person one by one. Our co-pastor went into the lake with Oscar and brought him to me. I took Oscar's hands and said, "Oscar, today is a very special day for you. I want you to have lots of faith because when you go under the water today, then come up out of it, *your illness is going to stay in the water. Do you believe it?"*

Oscar had been diagnosed with AIDS.

Oscar started to cry and replied, "Yes pastor. I believe it." We started to pray and asked God to extend His hand one more time. I baptized Oscar in the name of the Father, and the Son, and the Holy Spirit. Oscar was submerged then came up out of the water crying but happy and with the confidence that he was healed.

That day marked a difference in the life of Oscar. He began to prepare talks to give to people that were caught up in the same lifestyle that he used to have and who suffered from the same illness. I'm thinking that in the future he will be able to lead a program of AIDS prevention in the high schools and universities.

I know that God is going to use Oscar in the future and I have no doubt that he is going to make a difference in lots of people's lives. He will be a strong leader and it is a blessing to have him in our church.

Pastor Melvin Vásquez

For the Lord has heard my weeping. The Lord has heard my cry for mercy; the Lord accepts my prayer.

Psalm 6: 8b-9

Four years ago my life changed in a way that I never expected and was totally unprepared for. It continues to change, but in a positive way that has brought me to a strong faith, a deeper reliance on God and a desire to share my experiences with others. My name is Oscar Gutierrez and I am thirty-seven years old.

In 2004 I was diagnosed with HIV. I was not a Christian at the time. My lifestyle was not unusual among the young people in our community. I went to clubs, hung out with my friends and in all honesty did some things that I am not proud of today. I thought at the time that this was what all of my friends were into and I wanted and needed to be like them. After all, everyone else was doing it so how bad could it be? I guess that I shouldn't have been surprised with the diagnosis of HIV, but I was. And I was scared – who knew what would happen now?

It's when you become desperate that you start trying desperate things. With the thought of an early death swimming around in my head, I did what lots of people do. I tried religion. I went to a church for the first time in my life. It was OK, nothing spectacular or awe inspiring, but it didn't do anything for the deep-seated fear that kept rising up within me. No one from the church contacted me following my visit or followed up with me in any way. I didn't find this particularly surprising. I thought, "Why would someone from a church want to be friends with or associate with me? After all I have HIV and I hang out with a crowd that they would never want to be around". So, I thought that if there was a God, obviously He wasn't going to be of any help to me either.

Much later, my girlfriend at the time was invited by a friend of hers to attend the Más Que Vencedores church. She asked me to go with her and I agreed. What did I have to lose? This time I felt something different. I couldn't put my finger on it, but these people were different. There was something special here. My girlfriend didn't feel the same way and didn't go back. Shortly after that we broke up. But I returned to the church and looking back I know that God was directing my steps even then, long before I came to know Him and started to walk with Him.

During this time my doctors had me on medication to treat the HIV but I developed a skin rash as a complication and lost about 35 pounds. My weight dropped to only 120 pounds. I continued to attend Más Que Vencedores church and one night at a prayer meeting I felt led to pray. I spoke the following words to God: "God, I'm going to stop taking my medication. I believe that you are real and I want you to heal me. I am placing all of this at your feet. Help me Lord." Even though I didn't feel any different, I still believed and waited for God to work. It was round about that time that I decided to be baptized as a believer. I remember it was a Sunday and we went to Lake Coatepeque. God confirmed to me that day that I was going to be healed.

A little while later during a routine visit with my doctor, he told me that my blood work was better! He said he was surprised but that the medications were obviously working and that I should continue to take them. I had follow up appointments with more blood tests and scans. After each appointment, the doctor said that he couldn't believe how well I was responding and that I should continue with the medications.

Meanwhile, I had asked Pastor Melvin to add my name to the prayer chain. I explained the entire situation to him but we decided that all that others only needed to know was that I needed healing – no specifics were given to maintain my confidentiality. Within six months of being placed on the prayer chain called la Peña, my doctor informed me that my blood tests showed that there was no longer any detectable HIV! His first reaction was disbelief and the tests were all repeated but showed the same results. All of the doctors that had seen me were astounded. HIV does not get cured!! But they felt that mine must be an unusual case and that obviously the medications were working and that I should continue to take them.

It was then that I told the doctor the truth about my cure. I walked into my regular appointment with a plastic bag in my hand. I placed it on the desk and I told the doctor that I had not been taking any of the medications. Inside that bag was all of the medicine that had been given me at each appointment. I thanked him for all that he had done but said that he hadn't cured me nor had the medication. God had cured me!!

Since then my life has changed again. After discussion and prayer with Pastor Melvin, we decided to tell the congregation about my diagnosis and subsequent healing through prayer. I am very active in the church and I work with the youth in our congregation. I am helping them to realize that there is another option, to help them not get tangled up in the lifestyle that I found myself in. I work to draw them away from and out of a lifestyle that can have dire consequences. It is working and we are seeing more and more of the youth in our community connect with the church. When I see them share a glass that I have just used I realize that they too are convinced that I am completely healed – and we all praise God for his mercy and faithfulness.

I have approached the Department of Health in Santa Ana to see if I can get permission to work with people who have AIDS. I am excited to see how God will continue to use me, both at Más Que Vencedores, and more importantly,

wherever He needs me to be His messenger and worker.

Oscar Gutierrez

JOSÉ

*J*osé Salvador Sandoval is a dynamic young person who serves God with his whole heart. He is a fairly new Christian just recently baptized. José is a very quiet, humble young man who doesn't say much but he likes to be involved in lots of things at the church. He has a servant's heart and willingly does whatever is needed to help. He is a tremendous young man who likes to bless others.

José has one other very wonderful quality. He comes to the church every Sunday morning and without being asked he cleans up the church. He sweeps, dusts and cleans while the worship team is there practising and setting up. One Sunday he bought pop for the people on the worship team *and he has being doing it ever since. Another time he said, "Hey, you guys are going to be finished practising at noon and I'm going to be finished cleaning at noon, so why don't we eat together?" So he started bringing some chicken to share. Now they work and practise together and share his chicken every Sunday.*

It is such a blessing to have José. He likes to preach at the youth services on Saturdays and when he preaches, he does it with passion. José works in a business that repairs air conditioning for cars. His boss appreciates the fine qualities that we have seen in José and he treats him like a son.

José's miracle happened at one of our vigils. I remember that I was standing in the pulpit area praying over the people when José came up to me and said, "Pastor, can I come up beside you in the pulpit?"

I replied, "Sure, come on up."

José mounted the platform steps, stood beside me and whispered into my ear. "Pastor, God just healed me. I want you to tell the people."

"José" I said, "I want you to tell them yourself". And so he testified what God had just done for him. Then I placed my hand on his shoulder and prayed for him and he fell down on the floor under the power of God. As you read his story, you will be thrilled at the marvellous way that God healed him.

Pastor Melvin Vásquez

O Lord, you are my God; I will exalt you and praise your name, for in perfect faithfulness you have done marvellous things, things planned long ago.

Isaiah 25:1

Some people wonder if angels exist today. Some people wonder if God still performs miracles. Some people wonder if God even exists. Well, I am proof that yes, angels exist, yes God performs miracles and yes, oh yes, God does exist.

My name is José Salvador and I am 27 years old. I work as a mechanic repairing air conditioners in automobiles. I am not anyone special, just a normal average guy – so why did God take special interest in me? I'm still not sure but I am very glad that He did.

My story starts in 2003. At that time I suffered a convulsion and was taken to the hospital. The doctors did lots of tests but were unable to find out what had caused the convulsion. They thought that this might be a random occurrence and I went home and didn't really think too much more about it.

It was several years later that a family I knew invited me to come to their church with them. I was not a Christian at that time and had not been exposed to many people who were. I didn't know what I expected from the experience, but I went. I liked the service and the people and I had a good feeling while I was there – a feeling of contentment and belonging. The church was Más Que Vencedores and following that first visit I returned regularly.

About eight months after joining the church I had another convulsion. Again the doctors did a series of tests, but this time something showed up. The CT scan showed that I had two tumours in my brain and I was told that I needed to have surgery done as soon as possible. A date was set for me to go to the hospital. This was in October 2007.

At about the same time the church was going to hold its second prayer vigil. These are prayer meetings that start at 5:00 pm and last until about 1:00 am. It is a powerful time with many, many prayers being lifted up to God. During this particular vigil the elders formed two rows and those who wanted any type of healing or touch from God were to pass through the tunnel that the two lines of people made.

The elders had anointed their hands with oil and they laid their hands on people and prayed for them as they walked past. I walked through the lines and while I was doing this I suddenly saw two angels dressed in white with long flowing hair. They had their arms raised to heaven as they descended into the middle of the church. One of the angels came up to me and placed his hand on my head and I felt something hot where his hand touched me. He then moved his hand to the front of my head and it was then that I felt as if he was pulling the tumour right out of my head. It's difficult to put it into words but I was convinced that that was what was happening – that God had sent his angels to remove the tumour from me. Pastor Melvin said that he hadn't seen the angels but several other people at the vigil saw them even though they didn't see what they had done for me.

A couple of days later I went to the hospital for my scheduled surgery to have the tumours removed. I told my doctor that God had healed me and that he didn't need to bother doing the surgery. The doctor said, "Sure, sure, that's wonderful. Just put on this gown." I kept insisting that I was healed but the doctor was skeptical and continued getting me prepared for surgery. I just persisted though and at last he stopped and said that to put an end to the matter he was going to run some more tests. So, I went through all the same tests again. The CT scan showed that I had an enlarged vein in my brain but no tumours. They had an angiogram done that traced the blood flow through my brain and this test confirmed that the tumours were gone but that an enlarged vein was there. There was no explanation by the medical team regarding the obvious disappearance of the tumours. I knew what had happened though even if they found it hard to believe!

But that's not quite the end of the story. One night shortly thereafter at a service in the church I felt dizzy and fell to the floor. Everyone afterwards told me that I had had a seizure and that I was biting my tongue and foaming at the mouth.

It was the same thing that had happened early in my illness, just as if I had never been healed. When I became aware that I was on the floor and that people were hovering around me, I suddenly saw the Pastor's wife standing looking down at me and she said in a loud voice, "José, the Lord healed you. You need to claim that healing right now and not let the devil steal it from you!"

I immediately started testifying that I was healed and that nobody was going to tell me otherwise. Since that night I have never had another seizure and I know that there will be no more! But, there is more to my story.

The doctor that attended me at the hospital decided to leave El Salvador and to go and live in the United States. All of his patients got assigned to other doctors, including me. I was scheduled to go and see the new doctor for what I thought would be a follow-up exam but when I went to the hospital, the doctor said that my charts showed that I was very ill and needed to have surgery done right away. It seems that the original doctor had left behind only my old records and had not left any of the results of the second set of tests. I thought, "Oh, no, here we go again!"

I explained what had happened but the doctor just kept saying that he had to go with the records that were in my file, and those records showed that I had two dangerous tumours in my head that needed to be removed. Finally though, he agreed to do a new test. This was a procedure that I had not had before. An incision was made in both of my thighs, and wires with a camera were inserted up through the veins into my head. All I remember is how painful the whole thing was. It was only later that I was told what had happened. It seems that the procedure caused me to fall into a coma and now the doctors had to fight for my life. I personally think that the devil was angry that I had been healed and that this was all part of a spiritual attack. It was again by God's grace that I survived. Several hours later the results of the new test were delivered in an envelope to the doctor who was standing by my bedside. At the very instant that he was about to open up the envelope, I awoke from the coma.

When the excitement of my return to consciousness settled down, the doctor opened the envelope and reported what I already knew to be true, there were no tumours in my head! And furthermore, the enlarged vein had also disappeared.

The doctor's name is Dr. Oscar Manuel Vega Salazar and he has written a letter stating in medical terms that everything in my head is perfectly normal. I have given a copy of the letter to Pastor Melvin.

I know that the Lord has been growing my faith with this experience. I know that He has plans for me although I am not yet sure what those plans are. Most of all I know that He has healed me and I have been testifying to this – that angels do exist, that God is real and He is still performing miracles today!

José Salvador

MARICELI

A big blessing to our church came when Mariceli and Giovani Aguilar joined us. This couple has worked together organizing and preparing a series of home Bible studies with the express goal of training leaders to carry on the work of discipleship around the city. They initially came to us because of their interest in working with couples. We were having a series of Friday night potluck dinners for adult couples with an International theme...Mexican, Argentinian, etc. They were informal nights where everyone came in blue jeans. Sometimes we would have popcorn and a movie. Mariceli and Giovani just showed up one Friday *night and little by little became more and more involved in the church until they decided to make us their church home.*

Mariceli had more time at her disposal than her husband and she gradually reached out to help in other areas. Now, she works with my wife Dina to prepare Baptismal classes and she also teaches a Level One Discipleship course for young people. Mariceli is devoted to prayer and service to her Lord. She has also been given the gift of Prophecy and has been used a lot by God to bless and encourage other people.

Mariceli's daughter, Cesia, was miraculously healed and it has been a testimony of the faith and trust that Mariceli and her husband have in God. When Annette Vickers visited the home for her second interview with the family, Cesia was running a fever and had all the symptoms of her earlier serious illness. Although dismayed at this seeming setback, Mariceli and Giovani chose to continue to believe that Cesia's healing was complete. When God does something, He does it well. Therefore, logically, Cesia was healed though the devil would have us believe otherwise. We all prayed together, stood on the truth of God's word, and thanked Jesus for his healing grace. The next morning, Cesia was running around, laughing and playing and perfectly normal.

Pastor Melvin Vásquez

This is what the Lord, the God of your father David says:

I have heard your prayer and seen your tears.

Isaiah 38:5

I believe in the power of prayer. I have since I became a Christian but my faith has grown even stronger since I became a mother. I realize that most mothers offer prayers on behalf of their children, that many times a day "breath" prayers are said for safety, for strength or for health. But I know that the prayers that have been lifted on behalf of my two daughters were answered in a wonderful way by an amazing God. My name is Mariceli de Aguilar, and this is my story.

It begins in 2005 when I became pregnant with my first child. Cesia was born at full term, weighing eight pounds at birth. My pregnancy and her birth were completely uncomplicated – everything according to plan and no surprises. A perfect pregnancy and delivery, what more could any mother ask for. While most newborns lose some weight at first, over the next few weeks Cesia lost a total of four pounds and she was readmitted to the hospital. It took a series of tests before the doctors could figure out what was wrong with her. They told us that her kidneys were too small and that the condition was genetic. Soon her kidneys became infected and so full of pus that any surgery or treatment would have to wait until the infection cleared. She was so sick that the doctors told us she would likely die. We were completely overwhelmed – she was our first child, our perfect baby girl and now we were being told that not only was she was sick but that it was something that either her father or I had given her! And, now we were also being told that it was quite likely that Cesia would not live to see her first birthday!

We were sent home and over the next two years Cesia suffered with repeated kidney and bladder infections. She was always irritable - crying, angry and lashing out at people. We think that she was always in pain because of the infections and that this explained her actions. My sister and I had been members of Más Que Vencedores church for about a year. We always felt the presence of God in that congregation and were blessed to be surrounded by a group who believed in God's ability to heal. Cesia was listed on la Peña and although we were joyful to know that people were praying for her we had times when we were disheartened that she wasn't getting any better.

In October 2007 we attended a prayer vigil at Más Que Vencedores church. During a time of quiet prayer for my daughter, I felt God speaking to me. He told me that Cesia had been healed!! We went home that night and Cesia fell into a deep sleep that lasted most of the following day.

When she awoke, she was a new child. She was no longer angry or in pain. She stopped crying and lashing out. She remains to this day a quiet and happy child and her kidneys are completely healed. All of the church members have commented on her new state. They had grown used to dealing with an angry and irritable child and they marvelled with us in the change that God had made in her.

Our story doesn't end with Cesia though. In 2006, when Cesia was one year old and we were in the midst of dealing with her illness, the infections and her behaviour, I became pregnant again. The doctors were very concerned. Because Cesia's condition was genetic they fully expected that the problems that she had had would be repeated with my second child. We too were concerned. We struggled to deal with Cesia and we didn't know how we would manage if our second child had a similar condition. Now it was my turn to be placed on la Peña and prayers were being offered for me and my unborn child, as well as for Cesia. People in the church not only prayed for me but they anointed my swollen abdomen and the baby it held. I knew in my heart that this child was a precious gift from God and that He would keep it healthy.

The doctors believed otherwise and their fears were strengthened when an ultrasound revealed that this child most likely had the same condition as Cesia – her kidneys were too small! I put my trust in God and refused any other procedures or tests. The doctors expressed their frustration with my decision. I think they thought that I was crazy! They made me sign a document in which I accepted full responsibility for my decisions and that they were not liable if something were to happen to either me or my baby.

The prayers that were offered for me and my unborn child continued during my entire pregnancy. When I went into labour, a group of my family and friends met at the church and prayed specifically for a safe delivery and a healthy baby. Everything went smoothly and God answered our prayers. Rosia, our second daughter, was born at full term, a perfectly healthy and happy baby girl! The doctors were understandably perplexed but all of the tests that they performed on Rosia showed totally normal kidneys. They couldn't deny that Rosia was well but they also couldn't explain it!

Both girls are happy and healthy and I praise God every day for answers to prayer and for my wonderful family.

Mariceli Aguilar

NENA

*N*ena is my second eldest sister and although her real name is Maria Elena everyone calls her Nena. Because she is my sister I can say without a doubt that Nena has a very strong personality and very strong opinions. But that is not necessarily a bad thing! When Nena sets her mind to something, she does it with a passion. In the mornings she earns a little money by driving kids to and from school. In between she sells cosmetics from catalogues and helps her husband with his work. In the afternoons, she attends classes at the university. Then in the evenings, even although she is tired from working and studying all day, she attends the services that we have in the church.

Nena is very sociable and outgoing and makes friends quickly. She has a good singing voice and that, combined with her extroverted personality makes her a strong worship leader. It was no surprise then when she joined the worship team along with her husband. Having served in this capacity in their former church, they brought a lot of experience into our team. They have two teenage children, Raquel and Cesár Eduardo. The people of El Salvador are very influenced by American culture that they see on television, so since Eduardo takes after his mother in personality, he is the one who feels comfortable expressing himself with green hair and American style clothing. Perhaps not surprisingly, Eduardo's chosen ministry is to work the sound booth in the church. Raquel, the younger of the two, is involved in a team of young people who do dance ministry.

Little by little, God is forming a strong team of leaders in our church and Nena is one of them. Everything she does, she does with passion. She enjoys God and worships Him with her whole heart, hands upraised and a smile on her face. I have no doubt that in the future God is going to use her more and more.

Both Nena and her husband are faithful members of our prayer chain, La Peña.

Pastor Melvin Vásquez

Give ear to my words, O Lord, consider my sighing.

Listen to my cry for help, my King and my God,

for to you I pray. In the morning, O Lord,

you hear my voice; in the morning I lay my requests

before you and wait in expectation.

Psalm 5:1-3

My name is Maria Elena Marin and I am thirty-seven years old. My husband Cesár and I have two children, Cesár Jr. who is sixteen and thirteen year old Raquel. I became involved in what is now Más Que Vencedores church before the church was actually founded in 2006. My brother is Melvin and he is the pastor. I joined the church to support him in his new ministry but also kept up my involvement in my old church. Very soon it became obvious that MQV was a very special place and after they moved to their new building in November 2007 it was evident that God was part of this church. My husband describes the feeling when he worshipped in the place as nothing he had ever felt before. Here there was something special and you could almost feel the presence of God. Eventually my whole family became involved in the church and we decided to make it our church home. My children were attracted to the sports but they also enjoyed the freedom that they had to worship God here. I became involved in the women's ministries and now both my husband and I are part of the worship ministry as well. Since its inception we have been faithful members of la Peña.

My healing story actually begins fifteen years ago when I started to notice a lump on the side of my neck. It was not very big but I was concerned and went to the doctor to have it looked at. My doctors diagnosed it as an inflammatory ganglion on my thyroid gland. They assured me that it was not cancerous and no treatment was offered. Over the years though it grew to about five centimetres and was visible on the side of my neck as a lump. In the fall of 2007 my name was added to La Peña at the church. My request was for healing of the ganglion that had been growing increasingly bigger since it was first diagnosed. I put my diagnosis and treatment into God's hands through the faithful who were praying for the names on la Peña's list.

When we moved into our new church building in November of 2007, we blessed the building in a unique way. The congregation met at the front doors and split into two groups. Each walked in opposite directions around the building, offering prayers to bless the congregation and the church building. When we met at the other side of the building, we joined our voices as one to praise God for his faithfulness to this church family. Like the battle of Jericho, we marched around the building a total of seven times. I joined with others in the congregation to walk around the new edifice and pray for the church, for its members and for the community. It was a powerful night of prayer and feeling God's presence in our midst. While I was walking I felt that something was different. I couldn't quite put my finger on what it was, maybe just feeling God there with me, but my throat felt different somehow and I had a warm sensation on my neck. I put it down to the events of the evening and praised God that He allowed me to be part of it and to feel His presence and love there with us.

The following Sunday my son, Cesár Eduardo, said "Mom, the lump is gone from the side of your neck!" When I reached up and touched the area that had grown and become part of me over the past many years, I was so surprised when I realized that the lump was completely gone! My throat still felt different – sort of like there was a scratch or scar on the inside. I knew that I had been healed – that God had performed surgery on the tumour and had completely removed it. I was a bit concerned about the feeling in my throat but since God had taken away the ganglion I felt that the sensation was just His sign that something had indeed happened. I was sure that what I was feeling in my throat was the scar from the surgery that He had done during our prayer time for our new church!!

Several days later I returned to my physician for a follow up. I told her what had happened and although I think that she believed me she had to perform some tests to confirm it. The tests did just that, and the physician was amazed. She had been the one to diagnose me and now was looking at tests that showed no inflammation, no tumour, nothing wrong at all with my thyroid gland!! I knew all along that I had been healed but now had confirmation from my physician as to what had happened. To quote her "This is only possible because of God" – and who am I to argue with my doctor!!

We remain very active with la Peña. It is difficult sometimes to get up at 3:00 in the morning but once up, the time flies and it is a beautiful time with the Lord. And God continues to bless us and our church. My entire family have a renewed faith and it is very strong. It is wonderful to see our children involved in some of the ministries at the church and know that they will continue to grow stronger in their faith. Our congregation continues to grow and most of the members are young people, many with small children. It is wonderful for these young families to be able to experience God first hand, to feel His presence and see His miracles. We are indeed blessed and continue to give all of the glory and praise to our Lord. He is indeed an awesome God!

Nena Marin

GERARDO

*O*ne of the people who helped start up the sports'
ministry long before we became a church, was
Gerardo Marin. Gerardo earned our respect for his dedicated work and his faithfulness. He has stuck with us through
the good and the bad times. Now, he is one of our elders and
he helps in making important decisions for the church.

Gerardo has gone through some very difficult times
personally. He now works in construction but in the past he
had responsible positions in a couple of large companies.
However, a problem with alcohol caused him to lose his
money, his prestige, and finally his wife. He was left with the
care of his two young sons and is now working hard to renew

his life. Even although he has had to contend with these diffi-culties, he always has a smile on his face and always finds time to work for the church. We are all praying that he will recover his economic status and be able to move forward. If God permits, he will be reconciled with his wife and they will have a complete home once again.

Despite all his problems, Gerardo never strayed from God nor from the church. Today, he follows God with all his heart. He is a spiritual fighter, a visionary and a great servant of Jesus Christ. He is a great support to me person-ally and an inspiration to the other men of the church. He helps out by preaching at our prayer meetings and when he speaks, it is a blessing to hear God's words spoken through him. He is one of the bastions of La Peña and when he prays, it is with authority and power. He knows the God whom he serves!

Pastor Melvin Vásquez

But I will restore you to health and heal your wounds,

declares the Lord.

Jeremiah 30:17

Gerardo Antonio Marin Quintero is my name. I am forty-one years old and have two children, both boys, eight years old and four years old. I received Christ several years ago in another church and that is where I met Melvin Vásquez. When Melvin started up a sports' ministry reaching out to unchurched youth, I wanted to help. So many young people came to the Lord that Melvin decided to start up a church where they could feel at home. God put it into my heart to be a part of this congregation which was called Más Que Vencedores. Now, I am part of the pastoral staff.

My healing took place in November, 2006. The church had only just recently started. Ten years earlier, in 1996, the doctors found that I had kidney stones. I took natural medicines for a while, but I don't know if they really helped or if my body just got used to the problem. That day in November, 2006, I knew I was having kidney problems again. I remember it was a Thursday about 5:00a.m. I couldn't get up to go to work because of the severe pain. I felt so unwell. This continued until Saturday and I was supposed to go to the evening Youth Service, but there was just no way that I could manage it. There was so much pain that I could hardly sleep, even though I was receiving injections to relieve the discomfort every six hours. Nothing seemed to help.

So, since I couldn't go to the service, the founders of the church came to me! They gathered as a group, about six or seven of them, and came over as soon as the service was finished. They surrounded my bed and prayed for me for a long time. That night I started to feel better. I felt like something was happening inside of me. The next day I was able to get up and go about some limited activities.

It wasn't until Monday evening though, that my healing was confirmed. That day, I felt well enough to go to the regular prayer service. I prayed, "Lord, if you have done this healing, I want to have confirmation." I don't remember who was ministering to people at the front that night, but I do remember suddenly feeling something in my back in the area of my kidneys. I said to the Lord, "Father, I believe you are fully healing me because I can feel fire inside of me."

Whenever I had problems in the past, I made sure that I never ate chilli peppers because they always affected me badly. But, I was so sure that I was healed that I decided to test it out. So, I went home and ate chilli peppers! I had absolutely no reaction and felt perfectly fine. The Lord had healed me and I had my confirmation!

Since then, I have had absolutely no problems with my kidneys. No more pain....nothing! Everything is normal. I can declare that God has done a healing in my life! Prayer is the key. I joined La Peña one year ago and now I intercede for others in the prayer time from 3:00-3:30a.m.

Another interesting thing happened that you might want to know about. There were some problems in my home last year that I wanted prayer for so I asked the pastor if he would come over. He came, along with two of my neighbourhood friends who go to another church, and we gathered in the room upstairs. My wife and I were asked to stand in the middle and they laid hands on us and prayed. When we started to pray, almost immediately there was a release of a perfume in the air that smelled like jasmine. We asked each other, "Who is wearing that beautiful perfume that smells like jasmine?" But no one had put on any perfume or anything at all that was scented. And, no one had noticed this smell when we first greeted each other.

We continued in deep prayer with this wonderful smell of jasmine all around us. Pastor Melvin said later that he had also noticed a light cloud that had enveloped us. We continued praying for quite a long time. The smell was so lovely and it was a confirmation of the presence of God.

When we stopped praying, the smell disappeared! I treasure that experience and I believe that it was God's promise to me that he heard our prayers that night and that everything is in His hands. Now I can wait with confidence that everything is under His control and that He works out all things for good to those that love Him and call on His name.

Gerardo Marin

DAVID ALEXANDER

The Guevaras are neighbours of ours and it delights me to see their young son, David Alexander, running and playing with the other kids because for a long time, he just stood on the sidelines with a look of yearning on his face. It's wonderful to see him walking to school with his backpack full of his notebooks hanging on his back, and his young legs skipping down the road. The biggest thrill of all is to watch him playing soccer with boundless energy and unbridled enthusiasm.

It's such a delight because up until recently David Alexander was not able to physically do any of these things. Now he is like any normal child, running, playing and enjoying himself with his friends and just plain having lots of fun. He is a testimony to God's healing grace and an enormous blessing to us all.

Pastor Melvin Vásquez

This is the assurance we have in approaching God: that if we ask anything according to his will, he hears us. And if we know that he hears us — whatever we ask — we know that we have what we asked of him.

I John 5:14-15

We started going to Más Que Vencedores church because our oldest son liked going there. I am so glad we did, because I don't believe my third son would have received his healing if we had been at any other church. At Más Que Vencedores we learned how to pray and how to trust in God. Now I can testify to God's marvellous healing power.

My name is Victor Hugo Guevara and I am married, with four sons aged seventeen, eight, seven, and eighteen months. David Alexander is our third son.

When David Alexander was born, we really didn't notice that there was anything wrong with him. It wasn't until he was about a year old and starting to learn to walk that a friend mentioned to us that David Alexander didn't seem to be moving properly. When we watched him carefully, we realized that he was right. It was more than just being a bit unsteady on his feet, David Alexander walked with a definite tilt to one side. We decided to take him to the doctor and after various examinations, it was determined that he had a congenital hip disorder and his right leg was found to be 2 cm. shorter than his left leg. Without treatment he would never walk normally and the condition would worsen.

For a few years, David Alexander wore an apparatus that braced his legs. He had to wear it all the time and this was very hard on a young boy. He couldn't participate in any games with his friends and had to content himself with just watching. Our hearts ached for him. Eventually, the doctor decided that there had been no significant improvement and that he would need surgery. He was then assigned to Dr. Oscar Gomez, an orthopaedic specialist who is also a Christian, and this doctor said that David Alexander would need to have pins placed in his hip because the hip bone would have to be lowered and it would need to be pinned to hold it in place.

In El Salvador, when someone needs surgery or a special procedure, the family has to purchase the items that are needed. We are not well off and we could not afford the $136.00 needed to buy the necessary pins. In addition, Dr. Gomez said that as David Alexander got older, he would have to have more surgeries to have the pins replaced so that the bones could continue to grow. So, we started to pray. In answer to this prayer, our friends gathered around us and raised the $136.00 for the pins. That was a huge blessing and a great relief to us. The surgery was scheduled for September 27th, 2007. David Alexander was now six years old.

But meanwhile, my wife told me that she had received a word from the Lord that David Alexander was not going to need the pins. I would like to say that I had confidence in this prophetic word but the latest x-rays confirmed that the bone still needed to be lowered and that pins would be necessary. Besides, the scheduled day was fast approaching. So, like a good father, I went to the medical supply place to buy the pins. After all, God had provided the funds.

One day before the surgery, David Alexander was admitted to the hospital to have all the pre-tests and blood work done. We were nervous but thankful that Dr. Gomez was a Christian and we knew that he had the habit of offering his hands to the Lord before he operated. That same day, I took the pins that I had purchased with the $136.00 offering and gave them right to the hospital staff.

Of course, we were not allowed into the operating room, but we found out later that there was a lot of last minute confusion. The final x-rays were re-examined and then Dr. Gomez started the surgery. When he asked for the pins to be readied, nobody knew where they were. I can just imagine how upset he was! However, even more startling was when the Doctor realized that the hip bone that was to be lowered had already miraculously fallen into place! It didn't matter that the pins were not sitting on his surgical tray. They were no longer necessary! However, it was determined that some skin grafting needed to be done, so that part of the surgery was taken care of. Nobody could give an answer to the mystery of the pins and they did not show up until a month later!

There is another thing. Normally after some surgery, David Alexander reacted very badly to the anaesthetic and we were afraid that he might develop a fever and convulsions such as he had experienced in the past, but this time, he had no bad effects, and he even started to eat right away. Another blessing from God!

On Oct. 1st, David Alexander was still in hospital recovering from the surgery. Oct. 1st is "The Day of the Child" in El Salvador and quite often children receive little presents. That day, we were told that all of David Alexander's treatments would be free as a way of celebrating "The Day of the Child"! As if that were not enough, when we were leaving the hospital, the social worker came up to us and gave us back the $136.00 that we had spent on the pins that were never used! God has a great sense of humour. He is so good.

The doctor said that it would be a while before David Alexander's bones would be ready to bear a lot of weight and that he was definitely not to be allowed to run. However, it became impossible to stop him. He was so full of energy and he felt great. We even caught him bouncing on the bed. He could run and jump, just like any child his age.

David Alexander's name was put on La Peña's list at the end of August, 2007. I am the leader of La Peña and I was getting up to pray each night for the others on the list as well as for my own son. We found out that people from other churches were also praying for him. Everyone had been praying that David Alexander would be able to walk normally. We also attended many prayer services at Más Que Vencedores where my wife and I would cry out for his healing. Of course we gladly did this for our child. Abraham was willing to sacrifice his son to the Lord but God provided the sacrifice. Similarly, we put David Alexander in God's hands. God always provides for his children. He provided for us.

Victor Hugo Guevara

Author's note: Victor Hugo showed us the x-ray that was taken before the scheduled surgery. One hip was obviously higher up than the other and one ball joint was clearly smaller than the other. The last x-ray, which he also showed us, was taken in February of 2008 and it shows that the hips are equal in size and quite normal. And of course, there are no pins showing! Furthermore, no more operations will be necessary.

This interview ended with a mini-interview of 7 yr. old David Alexander:

Annette: "David Alexander, tell me in your own words what Jesus did for you."

David Alexander: "He lowered my bone."

Annette: "What can you do now that you couldn't do before?"

David Alexander: "I can walk. Run. Jump." (A little demonstration here!) "I can play soccer."

Annette: "When you are older, what would you like to do?"

David Alexander: "I'm going to play soccer in the league of Más Que Vencedores."

Annette: "Is there anything else you'd like to tell the people David Alexander?"

David Alexander: "Yes. I'm thankful God healed me!"

MIRIAM

*M*iriam is the mother of one of our parishioners and attends another church in our city. Her daughter Reyna asked for her mother's name to be put on our prayer list. She was in an advanced state of stomach cancer and things were not looking too good. I went to visit and to pray with her and was blessed by her honesty and trust in God. I promised that La Peña would pray for her and we would believe God for her healing.

Miriam has had a very hard life but she is an overcomer. She lives in a very poor neighbourhood but her faith is a bright light to all those around her. What struck me most about Miriam is the peace and joy that she has. No matter *what happens to her in this life, she is filled with the strong assurance that what lies ahead in heaven is something she can look forward to with anticipation. "Of course I want to be healed" she said, "but I'm ok to go to heaven if that's where the Lord wants me. Either way is good."*

Miriam`s story is an amazing one, but it`s her stalwart faith in her Saviour that blesses me.

Pastor Melvin Vásquez

In all my prayers for all of you, I always pray with joy because of your partnership in the gospel from the first day until now, being confident of this, that he who began a good work in you will carry it on to completion until the day of Christ Jesus.

Phillipians 1:4-6

I have been a Christian for many years and am a member of a church in Santa Ana. I am fifty-eight years old and God has blessed me with six children, two boys and four girls. I believe in the power of prayer and the workings of the Holy Spirit. My name is Rosa Miriam Hernandez and in May 2007, something happened to me that has strengthened my faith even more. But first I want to tell you a bit of my life story.

I am involved in a ministry at one of the regional prisons. This began in 2003 and I started by visiting prisoners. Over time I started to give them little gift bags with towels, soap and toothpaste. They looked forward to my visits and soon I started to share the good news of Jesus Christ with them. The prison houses over six hundred women and since my little ministry started we now have between two hundred and two hundred and fifty women who attend our regular worship services. Praise be to God!

I run a small store from the front of my house for my income and it supports me and my family. I use my interactions with my customers as a way to share God's message – I have been given this store as a gift from God and so want to bless Him in my work there.

Late in 2006 I was diagnosed with stomach cancer. This was a rapidly advancing cancer and I was told that surgery was too risky but that chemotherapy might be helpful. But, I wasn't able to take the chemo and the doctors told me that I wouldn't live more than a few months.

My daughter Reyna is a member of the Más Que Vencedores church and she told me about la Peña. I not only agreed to allow my name to be placed on the list but I also joined the faithful who got up each morning to pray for those on the list. Over the next few months I went through a strong spiritual battle. I felt that Satan was telling me that I was a bad person, and that I didn't deserve to be in the church, that God would never forgive me. I knew that my life had not been perfect, that my children had suffered through some things that I had been unaware of (both my daughters had been violated by a family member when they were young).

But I also knew that God was a forgiving God and that He loved me.

On May 15, 2007 I was up at 2:00a.m. praying. At 3:00a. m. I got the customary phone call that joins us all together in prayer. I prayed for those on the list and kept praying for about another hour. At 4:00a.m. I stood up and told God, "Lord, I am waiting for healing. I know that you can do it and I am waiting for you to give it to me". I took a towel, anointed it with oil and placed it across my abdomen. I had asked the Lord for healing and left it with Him.

Between 4:00a.m. and 6:30a.m. I slept off and on. At 6:30a.m. I felt a sharp pain across my abdomen. I was frightened and I called out to my daughter and she came in to where I was lying. I told her that there was something happening "here" and pointed to my stomach. She was amazed to see a scar across my lower abdomen – no blood but an obvious scar that had not been there earlier. She told me to go and look in the mirror. I saw the scar and it was one of the most beautiful things I had ever seen! I realized that God was at work and I felt so full of joy – just like I had when I first accepted Jesus into my life and felt the full glory of God.

That afternoon I went to see my doctor and told her what had happened. She was amazed to see the scar and I'll never forget what she said – "If this is the work of the Lord then I'm not touching you. Let's leave it to the Lord". She said that I was healed and all I could do was laugh! After about 6 months we had tests repeated and they showed that I was cancer free!!

I am absolutely sure that God performed surgery on me that morning in May and removed the cancer from me. He knew that it was too risky for my human doctors to do the surgery so He did it for us. He also left the scar as proof of what He had done. That scar was with me for fifteen days – long enough to show people what had happened and to testify of His greatness and healing power. Besides my daughter and doctor, others are witnesses to this heavenly surgery. The woman at the prison who leads the worship ministry, a lay pastor at my church and two other women from my church all heard my story and saw the scar.

But then in February of 2008 I started to feel some pain again. I returned to the clinic and was told that once more I had inoperable cancer. I am seeing a different doctor now and I told him about the surgery that God had performed on me the year before. He told me that if I had had the surgery in the hospital I would have lived for possibly three more months at the most. I am disappointed with the current diagnosis but I was cancer free for over a year and that has been a wonderful gift that God has given me. I am stronger now and am likely a better candidate for chemo or radiation therapy. I know that God has plans for me and that they are plans for good and that He can complete the healing that He has started in me if that is His will. Whether He returns to do another surgery or allows the radiation therapy to heal me or if it is my time to join Him in heaven is something that only He knows. I am trusting in His infinite grace and know that the prayers that are being offered again are being heard every day. I can honestly say that I will be contented with whatever happens.

Miriam Hernandez

Author's note: We interviewed Miriam twice to get all of the details from her story. At both visits we prayed for her healing and gave thanks for the work that she has done, for her faithfulness and for her joy in spreading God's message to those she meets. Miriam has a joy and peace about her that only God could give. It was an honour to meet her in her "little home store" with her parrots chattering noisily in the background. We will always cherish the time we had with her and continue to pray for her daily.

OMAR

You anoint my head with oil; my cup overflows. Surely

goodness and love will follow me all the days of my life,

and I will dwell in the house of the Lord forever.

Psalm 23:5b-6

This story needs to be told from two perspectives...we will hear from Omar Linares – a 24 year old man who experienced a true gift from God. Secondly, we will read the story from Pastor Melvin's viewpoint – the pastor at Más Que Vencedores church who witnessed the spiritual gift being given. We start with an introduction from Pastor Melvin.

God has brought some pretty terrific people across my path and into our church. Omar Linares is one of those. Omar is a neighbour of mine, living in his own little apartment. His family lives in the United States. He is quite contented living alone and is very busy right now studying religion in a local university. His passion is for the Lord. But Omar's Christian background was in a denomination that taught that the Holy Spirit is not active today and that miracles are from a previous dispensation. This was a bit of a stumbling block for Omar but he was still attracted to one of our cell groups (because of sports) and attended Bible Study faithfully.

In the past, Omar had a relationship with a girl, but it wasn't a good experience. His girlfriend abandoned him and he suffered greatly. I remember that he called me to his house and said, "I need your help." I offered him some advice and prayed with him. Some time later he said to me, "Remember when you gave me advice regarding my girlfriend Pastor

Melvin? Well, I'm so happy that I followed every one of your suggestions. I now have peace in my heart and I'm ready to move on."

Omar is the kind of young man that examines his problems. He doesn't try to avoid them, but faces them head on. He takes them to God and receives the solution. He is another great blessing to our church.

When we have visiting missionaries to the church, Omar is always the first to offer up his home. He prepares the rooms especially for them and willingly lends his computer and the internet, his television and his telephone. He offers everything he has and never asks for anything in return. It doesn't seem to bother him that he usually gives a lot but receives little back.

He drives an old Hyundai that is actually in very bad shape..but at least it runs. Omar uses it to get people to church and he never asks for help with gas money. We're always worried that one day the car will break down on the highway and that Omar will be stuck.

Omar serves in our football leagues. His job is to transcribe the scores and data of all the games into his computer so that we will have a record of all the statistics. He does it willingly and accurately because he has a sincere, passionate heart to serve God. It`s not a great surprise that God would choose to do something very special and personal for Omar to bless him in an unusual but very profound way.

Omar's Story

I live in the same neighbourhood as Melvin Velásquez and one day he invited me to play soccer with a bunch of guys from his church. Since I enjoy sports, I accepted. It wasn't long before they asked me to join a cell group and I accepted that invitation too. There was one issue though. I attended a Seminary in Santa Ana where I was taught that the Holy Spirit is no longer active in these present days doing the miracles that occurred in the time of Jesus. During our Bible study times, we would argue over this. I just couldn't agree with what the others were saying.

Then one day, the guys invited me to a Prayer Meeting at their church, Más Que Vencedores. These happen every Monday evening. The congregation believes strongly in the power of prayer and along with these weekly prayer meetings, they have prayer vigils regularly throughout the year. I sat in the back row because I didn't really feel too comfortable being in this church. Taking part in a prayer meeting was foreign to me and I wasn't sure how long I would stay. But, part way through the meeting I felt an overwhelming sense of joy – I have no other words to describe the feelings that I had. It filled my entire being and I had never ever, ever felt anything like it in my life before. I felt that God was opening me up. I felt like He wanted me to praise Him with my whole being so I lifted my hands and started to do just that. I have no real recollection of what else happened that evening but I know that God filled me up with joy for Him and that I worshiped Him from the depths of my soul. I was well into the experience before I became aware of what was happening. I eventually realized I was on the floor and that I was covered with oil. I never questioned where it came from – I knew that it was from God and that something unusual and wonderful had happened.

Pastor Melvin's Narration

The prayer meeting was like most others. It is always a joy to be in the House of the Lord and hear many voices raised up to God in prayer –it's like an outpouring of the deepest needs and desires within us, asking God to help us with our lives, our problems, our wishes. The sound of many voices raised at the same time to God is such a joy for me and I can only imagine how it pleases God to hear it as well.

Part way into the meeting, while in prayer, I sensed that a change had come over the church. I didn't know what happened, I just felt that God was present and I felt a difference in the group. When I looked up and out over the congregation I saw Omar in the back of the church – and he was shining. Yes, shining. There was a light emanating from him and it surrounded him. He actually glowed. I walked towards him and when I reached out to touch him I realized that he was bathed in oil. His arms, face, clothing, everything was covered in oil. Omar was saying something and because the prayers of those around us were continuing I had to lean close to hear what he was saying. It was then that I realized that he was speaking in tongues!

I immediately gave thanks to God for this occurrence and asked Omar if he knew what was happening. He didn't answer but jumped up and started to praise God aloud – in tongues! I touched his shoulder and prayed for him and he immediately fell down and then raised his arms and legs in the air and continued to lift praises. It was as if raising his hands wasn't enough, he had to raise his legs as well! I'm not sure how long he was like that but it had to be close to one hour and the entire time he was smiling and praising God in tongues. Others in the church witnessed what had occurred but they respected that this was something very special between Omar and God and did not interfere in any way.

When the service ended, we had to help Omar to his feet and take him home because he was as unsteady on his feet as a drunken man. But someone "drunk in the Spirit" has more joy and no hangover!

Many people have wondered why God would do this miracle for Omar. I believe it is because God had to show him in a spectacular way that He does indeed still do powerful things through His Holy Spirit in these days.

Omar Concludes

I have no recollection of Pastor Melvin being near me or speaking to me. I had no idea of the time that had passed and it wasn't until I spoke with other members of the church that

I realized that what I had experienced actually took place over several hours during the meeting. I didn't realize that I had spoken in tongues. All I remember is being filled with an overwhelming sense of joy and that I praised God with my whole being that night.

I still have the shirt that I was wearing that evening. It had been saturated with a fragrant oil. And yes, I still wear it; I haven't put it away or on display. I only own a few shirts and I need to wear them all! I do however feel the presence of God surrounding me whenever I put it on. I guess it has become my favourite shirt!

I am still studying religion but at a different school now. The one that I had been attending did not believe my story and told me that the Holy Spirit does not work like that today. Well I know differently. I know what I experienced and Pastor Melvin and the whole church can give testimony to what they witnessed that evening. My goal is to become a

Pastor so that I can continue to spread God's message – but mostly I want to live a life that is pleasing to Him.

YOLANDA

*Y*olanda de Carcamo married an uncle of mine who worked as a taxi driver. At one point he disappeared for three days and his wife was understandably very worried. On the fourth day his body was discovered in the mountains. He had been assassinated and robbed. He was the one who sustained the family economically, so as well as having to deal with the loss of a husband, Yolanda suffered in other ways.

When Yolanda started coming to our church she had problems in her arm, but she will tell you how God healed her. Here in El Salvador it is very difficult for someone with any kind of disability to find any type of work. Without a functioning arm, Yolanda was unable to work and provide for her family. There was just no way for her to earn an income.

Today, after her healing, she has developed a little business selling pickled onions on the streets. She puts onions in vinegar along with other ingredients to make pickles. When they are ready, she puts them in little plastic baggies and goes out every afternoon to sell them. God protects her wherever she goes and she is earning enough to look after her family in her little house.

Every Sunday and Wednesday she brings the pickled onions to church and sells some of the little bags to the members of the congregation. The people are happy to buy them from her and it blesses Yolanda.

Since Yolanda has been healed she has become a strong worker in the church. She acts as a greeter at the door and welcomes people with her warm characteristic smile.

It's a blessing to see her in action. She is a fine example of a single mom who refused to be defeated. Now that her arm *is healed, she loves to worship God with her hands raised in the air. She is very animated in worship and I get blessed just watching her.*

Yolanda has suffered a lot in life but she is a woman who wants to keep moving forward. She has been healed physically but has also received healing from her woundedness and emotional distress. We are looking forward to seeing her emerge as one of the leaders in the church especially in working with women.

Pastor Melvin Vásquez

I love the Lord, for he heard my voice; he heard my cry for mercy. Because he turned his ear to me,

I will call on him as long as I live.

Psalm 116:1-2

I have been looking forward to telling about my miracle. The Lord has been so good to me that I want to share what he has done in my life. My name is Yolanda del Carmen Salgero de Carcamo and I am 59 years old. My family consists of me, my brother Felix Chavez, my 23 year old daughter Elvia, and my grandson, Oscar, who is 8 years old. I want to tell you what the Lord has done for me.

Looking back, I can see that my story actually begins with a vision that I had where I saw myself in a bad accident. I wasn't a Christian at the time and I didn't understand the vision. But, a few months later, it came to pass.

On Sept. 23, 2005, I was riding in the cab of a truck when we hit a cement post. I was thrown out on to the ground and the post fell on my arm, severing the bones in two places. I was rushed to the hospital for immediate surgery. Dr. Giovani Gonzalez worked on my arm.

At that time a lady named Celia, who is now a part of Más Que Vencedores church, came to visit me in the hospital and I remember that she told me that God had a plan for my life. I didn't know the Lord at that time.

Dr. Gonzalez performed a second surgery on my arm and put in some pins. However, because the arm had been so badly damaged, it was still pretty well useless. I was hospitalized for two months then went into rehabilitation. But my arm couldn't bend properly and my wrist was very weak.

After the second surgery, Liliana Vásquez of Más Que Vencedores church came to my house and talked to me about Jesus. That was the time when I accepted Christ into my heart.

But there was still no change with my arm. It hardly functioned. I couldn't raise it. I couldn't hold anything. I needed people to help me all the time. I was especially worried in the middle of the night because if I had to get up, I couldn't manage it on my own.

It was determined that I needed a third surgery but no doctor wanted to be in charge of looking after me because they said at the hospital that if a third surgery didn't help then I would probably have to have the arm cut off. That news devastated me! I cried out to the Lord that I didn't want to be just part of a person. I wanted my arm. I started praying all the time…during the night, in the morning, in the middle of the day.

Finally Dr. Oscar Gomez, a Christian, agreed to perform the third surgery and I ended up with pins in my shoulder, my upper arm and my lower arm. My name was put on La Peña and I took comfort that so many people were praying for me. I was on the prayer list for almost a whole year.

As if all that wasn't bad enough, at the same time I developed very painful haemorrhoids. They were always bleeding. In fact, I lost quite a lot of blood. But I couldn't stand the thought of any more surgeries. With this new pain plus the very sore arm, I suffered from insomnia. When the pain was unbearable, I would cry out to God and tell Him that He was the only one who could help me. At those times, He would let me fall into a deep, restful sleep.

I continued to pray and pray and then one day the Lord gave me another vision. I clearly saw a room with four beds and yellow curtains and yellow sheets. I didn't understand it, but this time I tucked it away in my mind.

At last I was forced to go to the clinic to see about the haemorrhoids and the doctor sent me to a specialist. Since I wasn't able to go on my own, my daughter went with me. The specialist said that it would be very delicate surgery to remove the haemorrhoids and that it would be quite difficult to put me into the proper position because of my arm. He decided first of all to put me on a special diet to see if that would help, but he was convinced that I would still have to return to have the surgery. After that examination, I had to go to the bathroom, so my daughter helped me walk down the hall. On the way, we passed by a room on the right hand side, and my daughter said to me, "Look Mom, this is the room where they put you to recover after surgery."

It was a room with four beds and yellow curtains and yellow sheets! I said to my daughter quite firmly, "Well Elvia, I won't be here. I have already seen this room in a vision but I am not going to be a patient in this room."

Now I knew how to pray! I had no intention of being a patient in that room with the yellow curtains and the yellow sheets. I started giving the Lord thanks for His grace and mercy. I worshipped Him and thanked Him for the miracles I was going to receive. Fifteen days later, the haemorrhoids had all disappeared! Now I knew that the Lord was always with me. I just needed to call on Him and He would be there.

Meanwhile, I kept on praying for my arm. My faith was getting stronger. One time, in the middle of the night, my daughter had a crisis. She had been taking anti-convulsive pills but had stopped when she ran out of them. That night she started having convulsions and I couldn't get up to help her. So, I cried out to the Lord, "Lord, my daughter needs help and what can I do? I can't even get up. You are the only one who can help her."

Thank the Lord that He heard me. She was healed and the convulsions have stopped for good. What an amazing God we serve.

It was shortly after this that I started to receive healing in my arm. When I wanted to go to church, I couldn't manage to go alone. The pastor's wife sometimes picked me up in her van. Sometimes I would say to the Lord, "Lord, I want to go to church tonight, but if you don't send someone to help me go on the bus, then I will have to stay home." He always sent someone to me!

One Monday night, I attended the regular weekly Prayer Service. During the prayer time, all the women were praying for me....hermanas Betty, Lily, Mariceli. The pastor was also praying up at the front for me. Slowly, I started to feel that my arm was moving a little. It was like the muscles and nerves were being given more strength. That's when I started to receive my healing.

Another time a little bit later, at one of the vigils, I also felt the muscles start to move and I was able to move my arm in new ways. My dead fingers started to move. I could move my wrist more. Bit by bit, over a period of about 6 months, I received gradual healing. Now, I can cook and clean. I can raise my arm above my head. I can wash the clothes and I can hang them up. I can brush my hair. I can lift heavy things. I don't need any more rehabilitation. When the Lord heals, He heals well!

Now I am a member of La Peña and I pray for other people. I have lots of faith to pray because of what the Lord has done for me. This is my testimony that I'm happy to share!

Yolanda de Carcamo

ENA

I remember when Ena Pontillo was not feeling well and
I went to visit her in her house. She lives in a very
poor neighbourhood of Santa Ana that is considered very
dangerous. It is in a zone that is surrounded by gangs. The
air there is always tense and it is a relief when it's time to
return home to familiar territory. I wondered how someone
as pleasant and nice as Ena could live in such a place. It was
difficult to see her living in this community. But, despite her
surroundings, she is a living example of a woman of faith.
She fought hard for her healing and through it all, main-
tained her faith in God.

Ena lives with her three teenage children. Katerina, thirteen years old, comes regularly with her mother to church.

Eric is sixteen and plays in the Más Que Vencedores soccer league. The eldest is Douglas, nineteen. He is not yet in the church although we are praying that one day he will come to know the Lord.

When Ena comes to church she always looks happy and has a beautiful smile. She worships God with all her heart. She brought her mother to church one day and now she too is saved. That makes two prayer warriors in the family. Ena is developing rapidly in her faith and in her work for the Lord. I know we will be seeing lots more of her in the future.

Pastor Melvin Vásquez

I am the Lord who heals you.

Exodus 15:26b

"Milagro" in Spanish means "miracle". I am Ena Milagro Pontillo Diez, and as my name indicates, I have a miracle to share. I am thirty-seven years old and I have three children,

Douglas who is nineteen, Eric, aged sixteen, and Katerina, aged thirteen. I became a Christian in 1994 and joined Más Que Vencedores church in August of 2007.

My story starts on Sept. 4th, 2007 when Eric came down with appendicitis. He was taken to hospital and had an operation. On Sept. 5th, the very next day, I fell ill with fever and vomiting. On Sept. 6th, at 5:00a.m., my son Douglas had to take me to the hospital too. The fever and vomiting continued and I was bleeding from my nose. I had abdominal pains and my skin had turned yellow.

An ultra sound showed that a blood vessel in my abdomen had been blocked and then ruptured. I was scheduled for immediate surgery. The blood vessel was tied off and a biopsy was taken. We had to wait for one month to get the results. Meanwhile, I had to return to the doctor every five days to get the wound cleaned because there was lots of pus. It was not pretty! It was very worrisome because cancer of the intestines was prevalent in my family. Several had died from it.

Twenty days after the surgery, Ceci Marin, from my church, Más Que Vencedores, came to my house to pray with me. The Lord spoke to her and gave her a message that I would be healed.

When I eventually returned to the doctor's office to get the results of the biopsy, the doctor informed me that he didn't like the report. It appeared that I had intestinal cancer. He decided that I should have a second surgery to remove any cancer he would find and also to take another biopsy. Meanwhile my name was put on La Peña and the church started praying for me. I tried hard to remember the prophetic word from Ceci that I was going to be healed.

In the past, I used to be afraid to pray. Perhaps it was because I was afraid that God wouldn't always answer. But then one day, he gave me a vision. In this vision God showed me a lake with a big rock in the centre. A light was coming from the rock. God said to me, "If you give me your hand, you will be safe. I will take you to the rock. You will be able to carry all that I give you. I won't give you any more than you can bear. You are going to ask for things in the name of Jesus, and from now on, you will be able to ask for whatever you need without fear."

I prayed and prayed and I told the Lord that I wanted to live. I did not want to die like some of my relatives had from this disease. When the time came for the second surgery, I was confident that I was in the Lord's hands. When it was all over, the doctor said that he was absolutely amazed that everything looked clean inside. When the biopsy result came back, it too was totally clear. There was no cancer! I was so grateful to the Lord and to honour Him, I gave my testimony in church.

After receiving the vision, I wasn't afraid to pray any more. Now I can pray with confidence. For example, my older brother has prostate cancer and he is going to have surgery in a few weeks. I have been witnessing to him and telling him that with faith, he too can be healed.

Another neat thing happened to me. A little while ago, a preacher from Panama came to our church and we had services every night for a week. I went to the services and was praying that God would send me a job. At one of the services, the Panamanian preacher said that someone was praying for a job. I knew he was talking about me. Right then in the service, my cell phone rang. It was someone from a company that I had applied to telling me that they wanted me to come in for an interview. I went to the interview a couple of days later, and I got the job! I was to start the following month.

Well, I'm glad to have had this opportunity to share what God has done for me. I hope it will help other people. Pastor Melvin has taught us that we are all valuable to the Lord. When we accept Christ as our Lord and Saviour, we receive the gift of the Holy Spirit. That means that God is living inside us. When we pray for healing or for a special blessing, we need to realize that we already have the power of God at work within us. There is sufficient power there for our healing, we just need to believe it. It can work for you just the same as it worked for me!

Ena Pontillo

BRENDA

*B*renda Vásquez is one of my nieces but is actually more like a daughter to me. She is a very pretty eighteen year old with a beautiful heart. She is a chica who is never quiet...she always has something to say. It's no surprise to me that she wants to follow the footsteps of her mother and her uncle and become a lawyer. This year she has entered university to begin her studies.

Brenda has a wonderful voice and sings like an angel. She uses this talent to lead worship in the church. She also has a flare for the dramatic so with this talent along with her spontaneity and quick wit, we plan to include her in a new puppet ministry. We are excited about the prospects of using Brenda and other talented young people to develop a vibrant new street ministry incorporating these various skills and gifts.

Brenda's mom, my sister Betty, is a single mom and Brenda is a great help to her. There is no time for sadness to last long in that house. Brenda is always smiling, always moving. There was no father at her side growing up and she missed out on this support but God has always been close to her and her mom. In the future, I hope she will be able to use her voice to make Christian CD's. I believe God is preparing to move her to a new level. My prayer is that I will be able to see with my own eyes the blessings that the Lord has planned for her.

Besides all the creative talent Brenda also has a flare for sports. She really likes basketball, volleyball and soccer and takes a strong interest in extreme sports. She participates in Tae Kwon Do and a week ago she broke her leg from *a severe kick but learned a valuable lesson. Don't compete against boys!*

Uncle Melvin

I will strengthen you and help you; I will uphold you with my righteous right hand.

Isaiah 41:10b

Hi, I am Brenda Carolina Vásquez and I am eighteen years old. I live with my mom in a small house in Santa Ana. I guess my story begins around February of 2007. It started with a stomach problem with lots of acid. I couldn't eat because of the discomfort, the nausea and the lack of appetite. When I was on the bus going to school, I sometimes felt like I was going to fall over. At night I was often doubled over with the pain. It was terrible and I couldn't get any sleep.

I went to the doctor about it and had lots of examinations...an ultrasound, an endoscopy, and blood tests. The results showed that I had a bad bacterial infection. I was put on medication which was quite expensive and it made it very hard for my mom because she is going to University herself and we didn't have very much money. I hardly know my dad because he has never been interested in being around me.

But the big problem was that except for my mom, nobody really believed me. They would say, "Oh, that's just Brenda and she's always so dramatic!" Nobody really paid any attention to me.

It really affected me though at school. There is a person there, a teacher, who is in charge of discipline, and I was having lots of difficulties with her because I couldn't do my work, or I had to stay at home because I felt too ill. She really didn't believe me and neither did the other teachers, nor the principal. It caused a lot of stress.

I was only able to go to school maybe two or three days out of the week. I would go one day but would have to stay home the next. Or, sometimes I would be so sick that I would have to stay home for three or four days at a time. This continued on for several months. During that time I had several endoscopies which were always very painful. It came to the point that I was in danger of losing my school year, which was very important to me because it was my final year of high school.

My mom was talking daily to the doctor and I eventually got sent to a specialist. As well, I started seeing a school psychologist, although it was not someone from our school, but from a different school. It had been recommended that I do this.

The stress at school became almost unbearable. Finally the doctor said to my mom, "If Brenda continues even one more week at school with all this stress, she's going to have an ulcer because the damage is severe. And this ulcer is going to bleed and cause even more problems. At this point, only a miracle is going to save her."

We considered changing schools but that would really not help because the physical problem was very real and the doctor said it would probably continue for quite some time. Besides, my mom had sacrificed to put me in this school, which is a private school, and for us it was very expensive. I didn't want to just throw that away.

Finally my mom talked to me about having my name added to La Peña because it was getting very urgent.

Here, Brenda's mom, who was sitting in on the interview, added: "Everybody who knows Brenda knows that she can be very dramatic. But I, as her mother, knew the real seriousness of her illness. I saw her doubled over in pain night after night. The tears were not drama! A confrontation arose between me and God because something needed to be done. We believed that He could heal. I was practically saying that

*it was time for Him to do it. There is no father at home. The
role of father for Brenda has always been God."*

So, my name was added to La Peña and the church prayed
and prayed. Meanwhile, the doctors ordered me to stay home
from school and rest. The principal was not too sympathetic
and he said that I would certainly lose my school year but I
really had no choice. I just couldn't continue on.

My mom and some extended family members fasted
and prayed. I couldn't fast myself though because fasting
provoked more acid in my stomach, so I had to force myself
to eat. On Monday nights we would go to the prayer service
at Más Que Vencedores, our church, where my Uncle Melvin
is the pastor.

My healing wasn't instant, but bit by bit I started to
get better. After about a month of gradual improvement, I
prepared to go back to school. With missing so much time
off school, I had by now practically missed six months of
the school year. That morning, mom and I prayed together

before I left. Remember that this was a private school and it was very expensive for my mom. But mom decided that when God opens a door, no man can shut it. God had opened the door to let me be in this school, so we believed that He was going to make it OK for me to be able to go back.

That morning, the attitude of the principal was totally different! We were amazed at the change. It was almost as if he had been having the same conversation with God as we had just had. He asked about my health and how I had been, and my mom explained everything to him. Then he accompanied me to each of my classes to meet the teachers and he assured us that I would not be bothered by any of them. He arranged for me to have some extra make-up classes, and he set up extra exams for me, all without any expected extra costs.

By the end of the school year three months later, I was totally healed. By the grace of God I got 70% or higher in all my classes, even though I had been assigned automatic zeroes for the first part of the year because I had missed exams and so many classes.

This is all thanks to God and to the faithfulness of the church that was praying for me. I also was able to get a partial scholarship and now I am a student at UNICO, a local university. Right now I am studying Communications but later I would like to complete a law degree.

Brenda Vásquez

Author's note: Brenda is indeed a beautiful singer. She also plays guitar and is active in church dramas. There is no doubt about her flair for the dramatics! She is especially active in planning and participating in the Youth Services every Saturday evening. Brenda joined us in Nicaragua just the month before her illness, to help our Sports' Team do their Sports' Ministry. She charmed every one of us!

But more importantly is her obvious love for the Lord. Under the careful scrutiny of her uncle Melvin, she is maturing in her role as one of the worship leaders in the church and as a strong Youth Leader. We look forward to seeing how God prepares Brenda for the work that lies ahead. We are sure He has great plans for this lovely young woman!

BETTY

*B*etty is the youngest of my three sisters. (I also have two brothers and am the eldest of all the siblings). Since she was little, Betty always made up her own mind about things and it was very difficult to contain her. She always wanted to try everything. When I was a teenager I remember that Betty followed me everywhere and copied everything that I did. Since I played a lot of soccer, so did she. In fact, I probably played soccer with her more than I did with my friends. We usually played our games out on the dirt streets and people passing by would always comment about the young girl playing among all the boys.

Betty would play at any type of sports. She loved every-thing...soccer, baseball, basketball, bikes and even yo-yos.

Although I found my sister to be a little uncontrollable at times, there is no doubt about the fact that she is very intel-ligent. She studied hard in school and always got top marks. But, when she got older, she unexpectedly got pregnant and this completely changed her life. She was unable to continue with her studies and had to devote her time to working wher-ever she could to earn money to support her little daughter. It was not always easy for her but she never lacked food on the table. God always provided.

God has allowed me to have many experiences in my life, and I have wondered many times, just like Betty, how food would appear on our own table, but we have never ever gone hungry. I have learned a lot from her about trusting in God to provide. And He has never failed us!

Betty's strong character, coupled with her strong faith, has seen her through many hard times. She would do anything for her daughter. She is also fiercely protective of the rest of the family. If anyone were to explode because of something done against the family, it would be Betty.

Church has always been important to her. Even when she had no money for bus fare, she and her daughter Brenda would walk several kilometres just to get to the service. Nothing would hold her back. She draws her strength by having God at her side and she is a living message to the rest of the church. Betty has lots of plans in her head for serving God and I know that God has lots of plans for her.

Today, Betty is studying Law at the University. It's a good vocation for her because she just can't keep quiet! While she studies, she is earning a little money by driving a van part-time taking kids to school. When she is not studying or driving, she is working in the church. She is part of our music ministry and she does pastoral visits. Once she has her law degree, we're waiting to see how God will use her.

With her indomitable spirit, we are expecting exciting things for her life.

Even though Betty is an adult, she will always be my little sister. And even though we may not always agree on everything, love at all times, conquers all. It has been a huge blessing for me to see the joy on Betty's face when God responded to the prayers of this incredible woman.

Pastor Melvin Vásquez

My Shield is God Most High,

who saves the upright in heart.

Psalm 7:10

I am Brenda's mother, Betty. Melvin Vásquez is my brother. The Lord has done several amazing things in our lives but I want to tell you about our house. Brenda and I live in a very tiny little house at the end of a laneway. My mother bought this government-sponsored house with a down-payment several years ago so that Brenda and I would have a place to live. The agreement was that I would make the monthly payments.

Things went along really well for quite a while. I go to university part-time and am working on my law degree, and I have always managed to have several jobs to keep us going. But suddenly something happened that caused an immediate financial crisis. I hurt my leg in an accident and was on crutches and couldn't go to work. So basically I soon ran out of money to keep up the house payments. No one in my family was in a situation to help me so I finally went to the Social Services office to see if I could get some kind of assistance. When I asked what I could do, I was told matter-of-factly, "Nothing. The house will be lost."

Meanwhile, my brother Melvin had been praying and he put the matter in the hands of La Peña. He got the whole church praying too. Melvin believed that the house would be mine and he told me so. Even although I had no money, Melvin believed God.

Years before, the Lord had spoken to me saying, "You are going to pray and I am going to give you your own house."

"Which house, Lord?" I asked.

"The choice and the time are yours" He replied.

I remember thinking that this was a little strange, but it made perfect sense to me now. I knew that this was the house I wanted, and I needed it now! So, I set about praying in earnest.

I really wanted to keep this little house but to all appearances it was looking hopeless. I was also a little worried that if the word got out in the neighbourhood that my house was about to be foreclosed, someone would snap it up because it would have been a bargain and lots of the neighbours would want it.

For fourteen years I had looked after my daughter myself and had provided for her needs. I told the Lord, "You have always been with me. Always. You are my Shepherd and I will lack nothing. I choose to trust in you now." Right at the same time I was going through the problem with Brenda's health. It was a very stressful and difficult period but I made the choice to keep praying and believing God.

My family encouraged me to go back to the Social Services office. I honestly didn't feel all that confident about another visit, but I knew that God was listening to my prayers and that He would be working on my behalf. So, off I went. This time I had a meeting with a Christian man at the office and he suggested that Melvin buy the house. Unfortunately Melvin was not in a position to do that because things at his work were not so good right then.

The nice Christian man at the Social Services' office was keen to help us. He suggested that it might help if I could bring him papers that would prove that I had been working and earning money. I gathered some papers together, but I did not even have a part-time job to show that I was working at the moment. Nor, could I lie.

However, we put the application in for me to buy the house, even though I had no money and was not currently earning any. I don't know how I was approved, but on Sept. 13th, 2007, the "escritura", the deed to the house was given to me in my name! The house was mine! Not only that, but at the same time, I was given a cheque for $650 from the alcaldia for repairs now that I was the new owner! A man from City Hall went around to evaluate the house but I wasn't home at the time. My younger brother Jorge had the key but he didn't feel that it would be right to let the man in. The man just peeked in the window and asked a bunch of questions. When the assessment came, the house was assessed at $8,000 even although it had cost $17,000 to build. This was a house that I could afford to make monthly payments on!

Melvin cried when I told him that the "escritura" was in my name. He is kind of like Jeremiah. I have a lot of

Jeremiahs in my family! But, he never doubted that God would answer our prayers and that the house would be mine. He had also encouraged the whole church to keep praying.

So, I now own my little house and I will be paying <u>less</u> for the same house than what I was paying before! I marvel at how the Lord brought all this about. God is amazing!

Betty Vásquez

THE TWO RUBIS

*R*ubi *(pronounced Ruby) is the wife of the co-pastor of our church. I love to visit her house because she always hurries to make the pastor a huge cup of coffee, the size of three normal cups. If she has nothing on hand she will often run out to get me something sweet to eat.*

Rubi works a lot with women, I think partially because of her upbringing. She has always been very close to her mother, but it wasn't until she was in her senior years that her mother accepted Christ. Her mother really wanted to read the Bible but couldn't because of her failing eyesight. She has almost completely lost her vision. But Rubi sits regularly with her to read the Bible. She has read it so often aloud that her mother has now memorized many, many scriptures. They are both very special ladies.

Rubi has a strong, strong faith and is one of the strongest members of La Peña. She is in charge of one of the groups and helps to lead this prayer chain. She is also a big help to her husband and is known for doing everything with her whole heart. One day recently Rubi received a blessing to do even more for God. She was given the gift of healing. Now she is in the process of preparing herself to do a lot more with this special anointing. I won't be surprised if one day she will be serving in a big evangelistic and healing campaign. With her winning smile and willing, outstretched hands I know that God is going to do great things with her.

Pastor Melvin Vásquez

Do not be anxious about anything,

but in everything, by prayer and petition,

with thanksgiving, present your requests to God.

And the peace of God, which transcends all

understanding, will guard your hearts and your minds

in Christ Jesus.

Philippians 4:6-7

My name is Rubedia Lopez de Umaña but everyone calls me Rubi. My husband's name is Nelson and he is the assistant pastor in our church, Más Que Vencedores. I have three children, Paola, nine years old, Nelson Jr., six years old, and Rubi Jr. who is now three. My story actually begins with little Rubi. In April of 2007, Rubi started coughing and running a fever. I eventually had to take her to the doctor. She was diagnosed with bronchial pneumonia. The doctor sent her to the hospital for x-rays and it was decided that she would have to be admitted because she had some lung damage. I

149

was really scared and I remember crying a lot. She was so little and it was hard to see her struggling to breathe.

They did lots of tests and kept her in the hospital for four days. She was a bit better at that point and so they sent her home. But, just about every month it seemed, she would get sick again with the same thing. She was constantly on medicine. She would get slightly better, then, she would fall ill again. This went on for almost a year. We were so worried about her and I felt that she couldn't take much more.

Meanwhile, it was just about this time that Pastor Melvin felt that the church was going through a bit of a dry spell, so he invited his friend, Diangelo Jones from Panama, to come and preach at the church for a week. Nelson and I attended the services and on one particular night, I went up to the front at the altar, and Mr. Jones took my two hands in his, and he said that God was going to use these hands for His glory. He said that I would lay hands on the sick and they would be healed. I remember that he then laid his hands on me and I fell over under the power of God. I lay there for a long time with God's peace and joy all over me.

Pastor Melvin's note: When Rubi fell over, she started shaking violently and her body actually bounced up and down right off the floor, in a supernatural manner. Rubi does not remember any of this.

But, little Rubi was still sick. It was now the month of April, 2008 and Rubi had been ill for a whole year. She was coughing all the time and hardly was able to rest. She was constantly on medication but it didn't seem to help. Easter time arrived and during Holy Week, a Prayer Vigil was held. Nelson and I attended with the whole family. We were planning to take Rubi up for prayer. We could sense that the presence of God was very strong that night. When Pastor Melvin invited people to come forward if they wanted prayer for healing, we took Rubi up.

Pastor Melvin: The Lord gave me a strange message that I was to deliver to Nelson: "I don't know why, Nelson," I said, "but the Lord is saying to you, "Do you want your daughter to be well, or your wife? I know that the Lord is just, and I don't understand, but He is asking you to choose."

Nelson replied, "At this point I would choose my daughter."

Rubi Sr. continues: That night Rubi slept without coughing and waking up for the very first time in months. She also slept through breakfast, and kept right on sleeping. I was a bit frightened but I was happy that she wasn't coughing any more, and she seemed to be breathing normally. She kept right on sleeping till mid-day and Nelson and I finally realized that she had been healed and that God was giving her rest. So, we declared it aloud. Because we believed that the Lord had healed her, we decided not to give her any more medicine.

Rubi woke up perfectly well but we decided to make an appointment with the doctor to have the healing verified. Our doctor's name is Doctora Ana Ruth Flores and she is a Christian. We explained to her what had happened and that we had stopped giving Rubi the medicine. Doctora Ana Ruth examined little Rubi and after checking her lungs, she declared that Rubi was clean and perfectly healed. It was a miracle from God. That happened in April of 2008 and she has had no problems since that night at the service.

Following the strange word that Melvin delivered to Nelson about choosing between the health of his wife, and the health of his daughter Rubi Sr. *got sick and quickly went into crisis!*

Rubi continues:

My own problem began suddenly with a feeling that I had something in my throat. It felt that everything I attempted to swallow was getting stuck there. I was on the point of vomiting every time I tried to eat so I went to the doctor. The doctor said it was an infection and she gave me some medicine.

However, the medicine didn't seem to help at all and my throat got worse. The doctor said I would have to have an endoscopy. Someone had to go with me, so Nelson decided to come. An endoscopy is when a scope with a light at the end is put down your throat into your stomach. First I was given an injection in my arm, then, a spray in my throat. Then I had the procedure. However, something very scary happened. The doctor said it was the reaction of one in a thousand.

My throat started to close and I had a hard time breathing. I felt dizzy and my body started to shake uncontrollably. All of a sudden it was a big emergency! A whole lot of doctors appeared. I was put onto another bed and wheeled into another room. I felt like I was drowning.

I started to be afraid for my children. How would they manage without me? I was worried about Nelson too. Doctors were giving orders in loud voices. I was given several injections and something was clamped on my fingers. An oxygen mask was put on my face. Nelson was asked to leave the room because they were on the point of going to intubate me.

I was so afraid for my husband and my kids. All I could do was to call out in my mind, "Lord, please take care of my children because they're so little."

Then I clearly heard the Lord's voice. He said to me, "My promise to you is that I will give you strength. I want you to live".

I suddenly started to breathe and the immediate crisis was over. They put me into the recovery room for several hours and I got a little better.

Later on, I got sent home with some new medicine. However, it still didn't help the swallowing problem. Shortly after that I got sent to another doctor and prescribed yet a different medicine, but again that didn't help.

Fifteen days after I was released from hospital, we went to the Monday night prayer meeting at church. We prayed and prayed and prayed. Finally, a word was spoken out that I was to go home, that "my bed was ready", and that the Lord was going to give me a "blood transfusion." That message from the Lord also said that I would wake up in the morning feeling dizzy but that I was not to worry.

I went home and went to bed. I prayed, "Lord, I believe in you and I will conform to your will."

The next morning when I woke up and started to get up out of bed, I felt dizzy, just like the Lord said I would. I remembered His words though, and I wasn't worried. Then, I suddenly felt a jabbing in my hip, like I was having an injection of some kind.

"Lord, I know you are doing something inside of me" I said.

I told Nelson what had happened and that I wasn't going to take any more of the medicine because the Lord was healing me. And I was totally healed that day! That was the end of the swallowing difficulties. I have had no more problems ever since.

I'm so grateful to God for all His goodness and for the people on La Peña because they were praying faithfully for me.

Rubi Lopez

Melvin concludes:

I believe that the strange message I had to deliver to Nelson was to test the faith of the family and to strengthen them both for the ministry that God has laid before them. Nelson now preaches in a different manner. He speaks with authority and with a special gift. When he prays for people and lays hands on them, they usually fall down under the anointing of God. He and Rubi are working together in the church with more faith than ever.

Rubi is one of the leaders appointed to pray for the sick. Not much time has passed since her healing but she is already visiting the sick in their homes and praying for them.

Just recently, another little miracle occurred in the life of Rubita (how we sometimes refer to little Rubi). She had developed little wart-like eruptions that covered her face, hands and feet. Her parents took her to the doctor to have them cauterized but it seemed that when one was removed, three more grew in its place. They hated to see their child suffer so.

About a month ago, Nelson and Rubi brought Rubita to our Vigil night. They had decided not to say anything to anybody but they were going to devote the whole night to praying for their daughter. They prayed for hours with their whole hearts. This couple has learned how to pray with passion and strength and God heard the cry of their hearts. A couple of days later, all the warts dried up and fell off. Rubita was perfectly whole again! Rubi Sr. and Nelson testified at our Sunday service and encouraged us all once more. We have all learned from this experience.

Little Rubi is a precocious child who cannot be quiet.

She gets excited easily and loves to run and shout, even

when the pastor is preaching! I consider her one of the little

angels of God. She is going to grow up to be a beautiful

young woman.

This whole family has been touched by God. They are

precious to all of us at Más Que Vencedores.

CARLOS

*C*arlos did not have an easy childhood. His father died when he was very young and he became quite rebellious. It was a difficult time for him being raised by his mother and then by his grandmother for a while. He received money from his mother while she was working in the United States and this gave him status and privileges that few of his friends had. In time he lost control of his life.

Carlos will give the details of his story but thankfully his life was restored through Christ. He has tried very hard since then to lead a "normal" life and we have all seen the changes in him. He has had a radical change in his character and God is still doing a work in him.

While he was in school and dating his wife, Carlos was very protective of her and very impulsive. When someone said something against his girlfriend, he picked up a desk and threw it at him! He had been used to dealing with things by lashing out. Now, he is passive in comparison. Now, Carlos can do something he could never do before. He can listen.

Carlos, his wife, and their little boy live with his mother and he is a big help to her. He has great confidence in God and all of his family, his brother, sister, mother and cousins have all become Christians. We are certain that God will bring to realization all the promises in His Word for this family. Carlos is dynamic and creative and eager to serve God. I don't know if he will become a missionary some day but I know that God has great plans for him and for his family.

Pastor Melvin Vásquez

> *He lifted me out of the slimy pit, out of the mud*
>
> *and mire; he set my feet on a rock and gave me a firm*
>
> *place to stand. He put a new song in my mouth,*
>
> *a hymn of praise to our God.*
>
> ***Psalm 40:2-3***

I am Carlos Guillermo Ramos, twenty-five years old, and God has done spectacular things in my life! I am not the same person I was before because God has radically changed me.

When I was about twelve years old, my mom decided to go to the United States to get a job because we had hardly any money and it was very difficult for her as a single mom to look after a family here in Santa Ana. You will understand how desperate my mom was because she left my fifteen year old sister in charge of the house and she had to look after me and my eight year old sister. Well, no twelve year old boy is going to obey his fifteen year old sister, and I pretty well had the liberty to do whatever I wanted. I spent most of my time hanging out on the street corner with my friends and getting into trouble. My sister couldn't control me because she was just a kid herself.

The friends I hung out with, smoked, drank, and took drugs. I quickly learned to do all three. There was lots of beer, alcohol and marijuana. I wanted to try crack so it wasn't long before I was using that too. Mom was sending money and clothes from the United States but my money didn't last any longer than three hours because I used it to feed my habits. The money was never enough. I liked looking good in my new clothes. It made me feel like a big man. But the cost of crack was expensive and I couldn't keep it up, so I started selling my new shoes and pants and shirts to buy drugs.

This went on for about a year. I was so hooked that I couldn't even last one hour without at least some marijuana. I was always in trouble and one time I got caught by the police and was confined to the house. As you can imagine, my sister didn't like it. It was then that I even considered stealing the food money that was in the house.

I had two cousins that were members of a gang called "La Mara Salvatrucha". This gang is infamous in El Salvador. Everyone has heard of them because they are very dangerous. These cousins of mine lived with my grandmother and they had even more liberty than I did. So, I decided to leave my sisters in peace and go and live with my grandmother and cousins. It was a big mistake!

I would sometimes leave the house at 3:00 in the morning and would be gone for weeks at a time. I slept on the streets. Occasionally I would show up at the house just to change my clothes. I got into more and more drugs. I was drinking more alcohol than water. There I was, a young person of fourteen, hardly ever in school and high on drugs all the time. Much of my life was spent lying in parks totally drugged out.

After putting it off for two years, my sister finally told the truth to my mother and said, "Your son is lost. He is living on the streets."

My mother was forced to make a decision. She had a steady job in the States and was earning good money for her family, but she chose to return home to El Salvador. Now, she had no job, no income, and did not know how she was going to sustain her family.

When my mother returned and saw the state of her son, it had a huge impact on her. She couldn't grasp how this had happened to me. She wanted me to move back into the house but I didn't want to because I was afraid she would discover how really bad off I was. However, at this point I had no money and I thought that, well, at least she could look after me.

My poor mother! On some occasions she would be waiting up for me to come home...waiting sometimes till four or five o'clock in the morning. She would often give me a slap when I arrived but it didn't deter me. Sometimes I wouldn't even bother to come home.

At the age of fifteen I made friends with some guys on the street who sold drugs.

This seemed like a smart idea, so I joined them and started selling too. Now I was not only a user, I was a dealer. Now, I always had a little money in my wallet. But these types of people will do anything, even kill, to survive. Sometimes we'd have to flee the city to get away from the police. We'd go and hide out in another town for two or three months then we'd return when things cooled down.

I went wherever my new friends went. If they picked up girls, I picked up girls. If they beat up guys on the street, I beat them up too. I became close friends with one of them named Adolfo. Adolfo was braver than I so I started to watch and mimic him. If he slept in the street, so did I. If he didn't eat anything, I didn't either. If he fought, I fought along with him.

Adolfo had a good thing going dealing drugs. I remember when two young guys from another sector of the city came over to him to do some business. This was the beginning of some serious drug deals for him. He bought himself a gun for protection. It was a dangerous business. One time, an especially big deal went down, but as soon as the money and drugs were exchanged, a car drove by with five gang members in it. For some reason, Adolfo shot them all. The rest of their gang soon wanted his head and Adolfo had to flee.

I lost touch with him but it was well known that I was his friend, so the gang figured I knew where he was. Since they couldn't find him, they started chasing me and threatening me. This happened several times and it nearly scared me to death. Finally, they lost patience and said that if they couldn't find Adolfo, then they would have my head instead! I had no choice but to go into hiding myself in order to save my life.

Quite a bit of time passed and I was back living at home. My mother desperately wanted me to go back to school. She was even willing to put me in a private school and I gave in and said ok. It turned out to be one of the best decisions in my life. In this school was a pretty, young señorita and she had become a Christian the year before. Now she is my wife! Bit by bit, I came to know her and we developed a friendship, though I still didn't completely give up my old lifestyle. I had everything I needed....girls, clothes, even a computer....., what did I need with her. And yet, I just liked hanging out with her. She started to minister to me and eventually invited me to go to church with her. But, I wouldn't go. She tried to get me to go to house meetings, but I wouldn't go there either.

Then one day, a guy at school said, "Hey, I want you to play soccer with me in a league called Más Que Vencedores."

I thought, "O.K. I like kicking soccer balls. Why not?"

I enjoyed the games but one time a guy named Melvin Vásquez introduced himself to me and said, "Hey, if you want to keep on playing soccer in this league, you're going to have to go to church."

I said, "Nope. I'm not goin'."

He just said, "I'll see you in church on Sunday".

But when Sunday came, I didn't go. I went back to a soccer game though on the next Tuesday. Melvin Vásquez wasn't there. I played with the team and I remember that we won that game. Then the guys said, "Hey Carlos, there's a youth service at the church on Saturday and we want you to come with us."

This time I said, "O.K. I'll go."

That Saturday I went to the church and different people said to me that God had a plan for my life and that he was going to radically change me. I remember that when the pastor (Melvin Vásquez) preached, it was as if he was preaching right to me. I actually wanted to leave, but because of my pride, I couldn't bring myself to get up and go. So, I ended up staying and I listened to every word the pastor had to say.

Near the end he said, "If you think your life is lost and you can't recover it, I know someone that can do it for you."

I knew that message was for me, but I struggled inside and didn't want to accept it. However, God touched my life that night.

When I went home, I spent the night sitting and crying. I had a marijuana joint in my hand but I couldn't bring myself to light it. I wanted to shoot up some drugs, but I couldn't do that either. So, I settled for just a plain cigarette to calm my nerves.

The next day, Sunday, I knew there was a service in the afternoon at the church. I got out my best clothes, put them on, and arrived at the church an hour early. I stood off to the side and watched them put up the chairs. I waited and watched everyone come in one by one. Then I sat down and joined them. The service started with some singing and eventually the pastor started to preach. This time I felt he went on too long, and I couldn't really concentrate on what he was saying. I just knew that God was calling me deep inside.

When at last the pastor called people to the front, I went up. I stood beside a man who looked kind of official, and I asked him to pray for me. My eyes filled up with lots of tears. That night, I accepted Jesus as my Lord and Saviour.

From that day, my life drastically changed! My face changed. I no longer looked worried, weary and worn out. My body changed. Years of drugs and self-abuse had made me skinny and pale. Now you wouldn't recognize me as the same person. For several years now, I have had no drugs in my body. And I have never felt any desire for them, nor did I suffer any withdrawal symptoms because God did something in my life that I can't really fully understand.

My mother had tried to get me to change by slapping me, and by crying bitter tears. Family members came to counsel me. But nobody could do anything that would change me. Then God came to me one night, and everything changed in my life.

And as for the people I knew in the gangs, now I am preaching to their cousins and their kids at the soccer games. I go to a cancha in the same sector where my old gangs are with a bible in my hands, and I preach the gospel in front of them. I've even preached in front of my old enemies.

Yes, God has done something very special in my life. I'm not the same person I was before. This is the story I wanted to tell you. This is my testimony. I am a new creature in Christ because he lives in my heart. I am a miracle.

Carlos Guillermo Ramos

CODICIL TO CARLOS' STORY

As told by Pastor Melvin

Almost right after his conversion, Carlos became involved in leading a part of the Sports' Ministry. Every Saturday he would go to a designated playing field to share his testimony and the gospel with a group of young people, and then direct them in playing soccer. However, bit by bit, I got concerned that he didn't show up on time or that he would skip going altogether. He was becoming unreliable. Although I did not doubt his conversion and his love for Christ, his commitment and self-discipline could not be counted on.

I was at the point of frustration with him when I decided that the best course of action was to put up a photograph of him on my fridge and commit to praying for him. I set aside a portion of each day to seriously lift him up before the Lord. At other times during the day when his picture caught my eye, I would throw up another prayer for him. At the end of two weeks, after a concerted effort of intercession, I told the Lord that I was tired of praying for Carlos. I decided I just didn't want to pray for him any more, but that I would be willing to do anything else that the Lord required of me. Anything, except more intercession!

On the very next Sunday, just a day or two later, after the evening service, Carlos came up to me as I was talking with a group of young people. He was crying and then suddenly broke down and began to sob uncontrollably. He hiccupped out between sobs that while I had been preaching, he had seen an angel standing directly behind me with his arms raised.

Two huge wings spread out on each side of him, creating a frame around me.

He continued to describe that God had given him no peace in the last two weeks. He was awakened at night and would find himself prostrate on the floor. God spoke to him in an audible voice and it made him tremble. Between continuing sobs, he said that God had shown him things he could never describe and things that he just did not want to talk about.

"I told God to stop. I just can't take any more" he said. "It's all too Holy, too awesome, too grand, too....." and he shook his head, unable to finish.

I put my arm around Carlos and waited for the shaking and sobbing to subside. We prayed together then he went home.

The next night there was a knock at my door. It was dark outside and not the usual time for visitors. When I opened the door, I was surprised to see that it was Carlos. He said that he had been praying and that God had spoken to him again in an audible voice. There were more tears falling. He sat down, and in hushed tones, said that God had told him he was to go on a forty day fast but that he could choose a leader to go on the fast with him.

"And you, Pastor, are the leader I have chosen!" he said.

I groaned inwardly because I had just come off of a forty day fast a few days before. However, I had promised the Lord that I would do anything for Carlos...anything except for more intercessory prayer! How could I refuse? So, at the time of this writing, I have embarked on my second forty day fast, lifting up Carlos before the Lord anyway, because it is abundantly clear that He has something very special planned for this young man's life!

CECI

*C*ecilia Ramos, known to us as Ceci, is the mother of
Carlos. I remember visiting her house to evangelize
her. She was always very elegant and a lovely hostess. When
her son started coming to our church, she was elated. But
Ceci had an overwhelming problem. I prayed with her a lot
and helped her in her battle. Little by little she was able to
have victory over a crippling disease.

Ceci now works as one of His servants. She is a greeter
at our church and welcomes everyone graciously and with a
warm smile.

Ceci is a fighter, and like a typical mother, she has battled
for her children. For example, one time money was very

tight in the house, and without hesitation, she sold the televi-sion so that there would be enough food on the table for her family. Now, her son and his family, and her daughter and two children are all living in her house. She is like a mother and father to all of them. The whole family has come to the Lord, partly because of the prayers of this mother.

Ceci has recently bought a new van and runs a little business taking kids to school. Her son Carlos helps her out from time to time. I feel proud to know her and all that she has overcome. The story below of her miraculous healing is a further testimony to her inner strength and trust in God.

Pastor Melvin Vásquez

And the prayer offered in faith will make the sick person well; the Lord will raise him up.

James 5:15a

My name is Maria Cecilia Ramos Rivera, although I have been called Ceci from a very young age, and I am forty-three years old. I have four children, Carlos, Karla, Brayan and Stephanie. My story starts when I was thirty-five years old. At that time I noticed some pain in my shoulders – it hurt to lift my arms or to lift things. Over the next two months, the pain spread to my arms and hands. It was next to impossible to do anything that required manual dexterity or the use of my arms and I was in great pain with every movement.

I went to see my doctor, Doctora Ana Ruth and she was unsure what was wrong. We all waited and over the next few months the pain continued to spread until it was affecting all of my joints. The pain was constant and the list of things that I was unable to do continued to grow.

My physicians decided to admit me to the hospital for tests and after ten days and too many tests to remember, they diagnosed me with severe rheumatoid arthritis. The only treatment that was offered was medication that was injected to help me cope with the pain. In hindsight I realize that I was very fortunate to have a Christian doctor – I was not a Christian at the time and didn't really understand when she told me that if it was God's will He would provide for my comfort and possibly my healing. But now, I know that she added her prayers for my healing and my faith journey from our first meeting.

Meanwhile, my son Carlos started to play football with a group of young men. He enjoyed the time with his new friends and gradually became involved in bible study groups and then with the church, Más Que Vencedores. He became a Christian and he told me that he was praying for my healing and eventually he got me to attend the church with him. He also told me that since he had become a Christian he had been given a word from God that his whole family would be saved. He believed what God had told him and he was so very excited when I accepted Christ as my saviour. We added my prayers to those of my son and my doctor's for God's healing of my body.

By 2007 the arthritis was so bad that I couldn't walk, I couldn't dress myself or feed myself. I realized that arthritis is a progressively debilitating disease that has no cure, it just gets worse. I had to rely on others to assist me with all of my daily activities and I was in constant pain. I couldn't sleep, I couldn't do anything. Sometime in August 2007 my name was added to la Peña and others joined my son and me in praying for healing. There was a prayer vigil around that time but I was too sick to attend. Other friends and sisters and brothers in Christ who were able to attend were praying for me during the vigil. I put my whole faith in God and waited for Him to answer our prayers.

In the early hours of the morning I noticed that I wasn't having any pain. My son was still at the vigil and when he got home I told him what had happened. We realized as we talked that my becoming pain free coincided with the exact time that prayers were being lifted for me and my healing during the vigil!! God is indeed gracious! Within one week of that vigil and being added to the prayer list I noticed a gradual relief in my pain! My legs weren't as painful; I was able to move my ankles, then my knees. Within one month my joints were moving almost like normal – I could now dress and feed myself. I could move without pain and without assistance. My entire family was so happy and so thankful to God for His goodness to us.

The end of September I returned to see Doctora Ana Ruth. All of the diagnostic tests that we had done earlier were repeated. And, as she and I already knew, I had no arthritis - it hadn't just cleared up a little bit or even a lot. It was completely gone!!

I will forever be grateful to my son Carlos who brought me to the church and to a faith in God. And to those who ministered to Carlos and taught him about the wonderful God who loved him. God has proven very faithful to me and my family. He answered our prayers and provided complete healing of my disease. My youngest daughter Stephanie realized that something amazing had occurred and she told me that she "wanted to go to Melvin's church" too. Now my entire family attends regularly and we are very faithful in prayer as we have learned first hand about God's faithfulness to us.

I know that I was healed by God because of the prayers that were being offered by those who pray faithfully and sacrificially for those names on la Peña. And I will be forever grateful to God for giving me back my health. I continue to have a strong prayer life and hope that in some small way my prayers can bring healing to someone else who is in need.

Cecilia Ramos

Author's note: Ceci graciously offered to drive us around in her van when we went around doing the interviews. It wasn't until we were almost finished that she shyly told us that she too had a healing story to share. We would never have guessed that she had only recently been crippled up by arthritis! Ceci is very active in the church and is quick to pray for others.

YANIRA

*I*n her story of God's healing Yanira does not mention the fascinating beginning of her life. Ever since she was little, Yanira was always sick. Her immune system was constantly battling off some type of illness. Her family lived in a small pueblo in El Salvador called Coatepeque far away from any Health Centre where she might have been able to get some help. When she was only six months old she had a crisis. She became very ill and each day she got worse and worse until one day while her mother held her in her arms, she died.

Near the house was a Catholic church and Yanira's mother, Tinita, rushed the baby to the priest. She presented the dead child and begged the priest to baptize her. The priest granted her request and at the very moment when he poured the water on the baby's head, the child gave a deep sigh and started to breathe. From that moment the mother knew that God had something special planned for this child and she devoted herself to prayer and thanksgiving for the life of her daughter, Yanira.

But as Yanira grew up with her two sisters, she was the one who always seemed to get sick. Her mother kept a watchful eye on her and kept on praying. Yanira met her husband José while they were in High School and after dating for five years they decided to get married and start a home together. But her frequent illnesses continued to plague her.

Nonetheless, Yanira was blessed with many of the same characteristics as her mother, intelligent, kind, attentive, and strong in her faith. She learned how to fight for her children *just like her mother did before her, and now she will tell you*

her own story of another miraculous healing.

Pastor Melvin Vásquez

Do not be anxious about anything,

but in everything, by prayer and petition, with

thanksgiving, present your requests to God. And the peace

of God, which transcends all understanding,

will guard your hearts and minds in Christ Jesus.

Philippians 4:6-7

I am thirty-nine years old and have been blessed with three beautiful children. I realize that all children are a gift from God but I believe that my children are not only a gift but a miracle that He has given my husband and me. Kevin is thirteen years old, Nathalia is four years old and my miracle baby, Fernando is just eleven months old. My first two pregnancies were difficult and I had a lot of complications including pre-eclampsia. This is a condition sometimes referred to as pregnancy-induced hypertension. It is defined by high blood pressure and excess protein in the urine. The changes in blood pressure change the blood flow to the baby while in utero. Without proper blood flow, the baby could be born small or with some serious complications due to insufficient nutrients and oxygen while in utero. While not always life threatening, this is a risk for both the mother and baby and complications are highest when the situation presents early in a pregnancy and then in subsequent pregnancies.

On the day that Kevin (my eldest) was born the doctors said that I almost died as my blood pressure was dangerously high. When I got pregnant for the second time and again developed pre-eclampsia everyone was worried. Following Nathalia's birth I again was very hypertensive and I was actually blind for about two months. Changes in vision are not unusual with pre-eclampsia, but they don't usually last for two months. I couldn't move my legs and I had rehabilitation exercises for my limbs for almost eighteen months following the baby's birth. Nathalia had complications as well, her legs developed very slowly and she was very slow in learning to walk. When I finally regained my sight, I was told that we should not even consider having another child because if we did either the baby or I - or both of us – would likely die. I had not been well even before my pregnancies and had a history of asthma and a heart lesion that they termed cardiomyopathy. Neither was very serious on their own but in combination with high blood pressure and the other effects of pre-eclampsia I knew that the doctors were right to warn us against another pregnancy.

It was around this time that I accepted Christ as my saviour. My sister had been attending Más Que Vencedores church for several months. At first I wasn't interested because I thought that it was a just a church for the youth. They were very involved in soccer and I didn't think that it was a "real church". But all that changed.

Very early in 2007 I realized that I was pregnant for a third time. This was totally unplanned and a surprise for my husband and I. My doctors were understandably concerned. They felt that the risk of a cardiac infarction (heart attack) was very possible and they were preparing themselves, my husband and me for what they called a "catastrophe"! At first the pregnancy developed normally, except that I was very nauseated. Because of the nausea, I wasn't eating properly so became malnourished. Although I was a Christian I did not feel that I was "walking with God". I decided to change churches and joined my sister and her family at Más Que Vencedores church. By this time they were worshiping in a real building and it was more than just a "youth church". I felt my faith grow as I began to develop a stronger relationship with God. My name was added to la Peña and I felt good knowing that others were praying for me.

At seven months gestation I was admitted to the hospital. My blood pressure was very high and the doctors told my husband that most likely the baby would not survive and that possibly I would not either. My family and friends left my side at the hospital to go to the church to pray for me. As I started into labour, with every contraction my blood pressure increased. It was during this time, during my worst contractions, that I fell into a deep sleep – without anaesthetic or any other medications. I knew later that God had done this for me and that He was in control and would look after us. I actually slept while my cervix dilated from 4 to 9 cms! The nurses on staff were totally amazed that I was sleeping through the contractions – and in fact didn't even realize that I was having them!

During the last hour prior to Fernando's birth the doctor who was supposed to be on call and do the delivery was not available. To my surprise (and delight) Dr Gutierrez arrived – someone that I knew from the church, someone who was also a Christian, and someone who knew me and understood my faith.

Fernando was born weighing 4 lbs and except for being small, he was perfectly healthy. I had no complications with the delivery besides the blood pressure during the contractions and no complications following the birth. When my first son, Kevin, was born I was in bed for eight days and had lost my vision for over one month. With Nathalia I was bedridden for two days and couldn't see for two months. With Fernando (and mostly with God's help) I was perfectly fine, some minor eye irritation but nothing complicated.

I know that the prayers lifted on my behalf brought God to intercede and keep Fernando and me safe. Since his birth I have felt totally reconnected with God and I now have an even deeper faith and reliance on him. My asthma has been completely under control – without medications. My cardio-myopathy has completely resolved – all of my tests have been negative and there was no damage done during the delivery because of the blood pressure.

I give thanks and praise to God every day that He has blessed me with such a wonderful family. My children continue to be a blessing to my husband and me. My church family held us up in prayer and continue to be supportive and there when we need them. But my biggest blessing is being part of the family of God and being able to receive all that He has to give me.

Yanira de Garcia

REYNA

*R*eyna is a woman who enjoys the favour of God in her life and she is a testimony to the rest of us that the promises of God will become a reality for each one of us in His perfect timing. This does not mean that Reyna has had an easy life. On the contrary, she faced many trials and tribulations that would have defeated many people. Even although Reyna did not have a strong personal relationship with the Lord during her struggles, she knew enough to turn to Him in her despair. She was not disappointed.

Pastor Melvin Vásquez

But you are a shield around me, O Lord; you bestow glory

on me and lift up my head. To the Lord I cry aloud,

and he answers me from his holy hill.

Psalm 3:3-4

I am Reyna Isabel Martinez de Gil. I have a loving husband, Alberto and two sons, Luis who is nineteen years old and César who is sixteen. But, Alberto was not always the ideal husband. In fact, when I married him, he was actually an alcoholic. Shortly after our marriage things went from bad to worse and my life was filled with worries, arguments, battles, and beatings.

The 12th of March, 2001, was a very difficult night for me. I was mistreated and badly beaten by my husband and my oldest son Luis was present to witness it. Luis cried and cried watching his dad hit his mom without pity. The following morning I gathered together some necessities and along with my two sons, then nine and twelve years old,

I left the house. That day I mentally threw in the garbage fifteen long years of marriage filled with pain and suffering. I couldn't take it any more.

For six months I lived far away from my husband but somehow he found out where we were. One night, he arrived at our home drunk and with a gun in his hand. He put it to my head and said that if I did not return with him, he would shoot me. He then took my two sons and put them in the car. The phone rang and Luis and César were on their dad's cell phone crying and crying, and saying that their dad said he would kill them if I didn't return with him and that their deaths would be on my conscience. I knew that I couldn't go with Alberto because he would have killed me but I feared for my children. My sons who had been my strength and help were now my torture.

My husband drove away with my boys and I had no peace until I heard from some family members that they were safe. Tired, alone, and with my body still suffering from past beatings I fell into a stage of depression. I couldn't eat for the overwhelming sadness I bore. My days were spent crying alone in my room. Finally, one day, I decided I would go to the United States to try and seek a better life. It meant I would be leaving behind my most precious possessions, my children, but they were lost to me anyway. There was no future for me in El Salvador. My hope was to earn some money in the United States and then return for my boys. And so, I left without any money, without any food, and with just a few clothes.

I first crossed through Guatemala and Mexico, taking little jobs along the way as a house servant, working in the fields, or packing in factories. Little by little I moved my way closer to the U.S. border. At one point I suffered a cerebral haemorrhage and was grateful to God that some people found me and helped me. Eight months passed with me not knowing anything about my family or my children. When at last I reached the river bordering the US, the only way across was to swim. I tried to do it, as I suppose so many other people have tried, but I almost drowned in the process. Defeated, I had no option but to return to El Salvador.

When I arrived at the frontier I was alone and the few things that I had taken with me had long ago been stolen. Even the little book where I had written down all the phone numbers of the people I knew in El Salvador was gone. I could not remember any of the phone numbers except one, the phone number of the man who had scarred my life, the phone number of my husband.

Reluctantly, I called him and he agreed to come and pick me up. He took me to the house where he was living and I was ecstatic to be reunited with my eldest son Luis. (César was living with one of my sisters). This marked the key turning point in our lives. Never again did my husband hit me and miraculously we formed a little family again, this time a happy one.

Two years passed and our oldest son started attending a church. One year later, the four of us were going regularly to Sunday services. In the residencial area where we lived, I got to know a precious lady name Lily. She is used mightily by God with a gift of prophecy and she was God's instrument to give us God's promises that seemed impossible at the time, but which injected us with hope and encouragement. Through Lily, we all gave our hearts to the Lord. Bit by bit we learned more about the Bible and we matured as Christians.

One day we learned about the Más Que Vencedores Sports Church and we decided to start attending there. It has turned out to be a huge blessing and God has permitted us to grow in our faith, serve Him in ministry and to walk in His favour.

My husband was a shareholder in a car repair business along with several of his many brothers. But one day there was a disagreement and the other shareholders decided to remove my husband from the business. Difficult days followed with no money, no food and no resources to send our children to school. But we stood on the promises of God that we had received through Lily, plus the promises that God gives his children in the Bible. It had been prophesied that we would prosper economically so we knew that God would not forget us.

Ten months passed without any significant changes but we stood firm on God's word. A Christian lawyer was helping us and we won the lawsuit that my husband had launched. The money we received was sufficient for my husband to start up his own small mechanics business. Now we live in a different location and we are prospering economically, just as the Lord said we would. Our home is now a home where peace and tranquility reign and we are filled with the joy of the Lord. Truly we are a family full of miracles. But my story doesn't end here. I also want to share about a physical healing that took place.

It was in May 2007 when I first noticed something wrong around my rectum. I thought that I had been bitten by something. Over the next few days it got larger and inflamed and eventually it burst and what came out was a mixture of blood and pus. I thought that that was the end of it, whatever it was it had gone now and I would be fine. Well, that's wasn't quite the case.

A few weeks later I felt the return of what I thought was an infection. I went to my doctor, Doctora Karina de Sandoval, and she told me that indeed I had an infection and gave me antibiotics. The swelling came and went and with that came headaches and fevers. No one really knew what was wrong with me and I was embarrassed to tell anyone so the only person besides my husband who knew how I was feeling was my friend Liliana.

Eventually my doctor diagnosed a fistula. Besides antibiotics, my doctor gave me some creams to use but she said that there was nothing more that could be done for it except to have repeated surgeries. They would be necessary but would not solve the problem because eventually no more surgeries would be able to be done. She said that the opening would continue to get bigger and bigger. This news upset me. I had also been through surgeries before. It was not an experience that I wanted to repeat!

So, I reached out to God and we stayed faithful in prayer. Soon after joining the Más Que Vencedores church our family was listed on la Peña for economic reasons. When I started to have more medical problems I spoke with Pastor Melvin and my name was added to la Peña specifically for prayer for healing. I had a towel that had been anointed with oil and I regularly applied it when I arose for prayer at 3:00 am. Yes, not only was my name on la Peña but I was one of the faithful who got up in the early morning hours to pray for the others whose names were also on la Peña. On Monday nights the church holds regular prayer nights. During one of these I heard testimonies from people who had received answers to their prayers for healing and I asked God, "Why not me?" I was not sure why God did not choose to heal me at that time but I placed it all in His hands and waited for His timing.

Lily had told an American friend about my illness and this lady offered money to send me to more doctors and have more tests done. I refused at first but then I decided to accept just in case it was part of God's plan for my healing. This new doctor confirmed that my problem was not cancer but that I did indeed have a fistula and that I would need to have surgery right away. The problem was that the surgery would cost $1300 and with my husband out of work at the time, we couldn't afford the operation. As well, he said that the surgery would not be a cure, that very likely I would need more surgeries and that I might end up with a colostomy – a plastic bag attached to my colon that would take the place of my rectum. None of this sounded like something that I wanted to do and even if I had wanted to go through with the recommendations we could not afford even the first of the operations.

I went to Pastor Melvin and explained the situation and we told those on la Peña the specifics regarding my prayer needs. Then in September 2007 I attended a prayer vigil at Más Que Vencedores. During the vigil the elders stood in two lines facing each other, making a "healing tunnel" with their hands raised upwards to God. First the children passed through for a blessing, then the youth, then the adults. As they went through many were crying. Many raised their hands in worship to God. Then the elders asked those who needed healing to pass through but I did not go up. I sat in the back of the church with my husband and even though I wanted to go through that bridge for healing I was feeling too unwell to even walk up to the front of the church!

As I sat there, I suddenly felt a pain in my shoulder, like I had a heavy weight pressing there. It hurt sufficiently that I dug my nails into my hands to help relieve some of the pain.

Then I realized that someone from the church had come up behind me and had laid their hand on my shoulder and was praying for me. It was Pastor Melvin. I heard him pray "Lord, this is your time for healing. Lord, heal your servant Reyna!" I also heard Liliana's voice lifted in prayer for my healing. As I sat there I felt like something was being pulled out from inside of me. That's the only way I can describe it. Afterwards when explaining this to Lily, she told me that she had felt the same pain. She said that during her experience with the pain, she had heard God speak concerning me. He told her that he would do three surgeries on me over the next few days. I should go home and rest for three days, drink lots of water and fast and pray.

Over those next three days I felt an incredible peace. But I also felt some physical changes. I felt like I was being stitched up, like an incision being closed up after a surgery. I think that God gave me these physical sensations as a demonstration that I was indeed being healed – that He was doing the surgery and closing up the wounds for me. I took no medication during this time and I trusted that God had done what He said He would. When I was bathing I purposely did not feel for any changes because I wanted to put my total trust in the Lord. After four days I did check where the fistula had been and I felt nothing – God had indeed healed me!

But that is not quite the end of it. Several weeks passed then one day I felt something again. I touched that area and sure enough there was a return of the lesion. But I prayed and prayed when that happened because I knew that it was the evil one who wanted to turn me from my faith and trust in God. I made a conscious decision to not testify to a lie because it would give a voice to Satan. I chose to believe that God had healed me so I rebuked Satan and stood on God's word. God is faithful and the next time I reached back to check, the lesion was gone. Since the beginning of 2008 I have felt no return of the fistula and my doctors are amazed that I have been healed.

I believe that God not only healed the fistula, but that He is continuing to keep me safe and healthy. Now my entire family are Christians and they have stories of their own that they could share. We all believe that we are a work of God, beloved children of His.

My family and I have gone through many experiences. Looking back, even to the days before I really knew him, I know that God has always been watching over us and that He has proven himself over and over to be a reality in our lives. I hope that my story will help others to trust in our loving Heavenly Father.

Reyna de Gil

LILY

*L*ily is my sister and the oldest of my siblings. As a child, she was always very serious and took on the role of micro-managing her younger brothers and sisters. She was the one who helped bring order into our household. As a teenager, she was not very interested in boys or in going out with her friends. Instead, she dedicated herself to her studies. She trained as a nurse after graduating from high school but didn't really serve in this profession, preferring instead to devote herself full-time to serving the Lord.

Lily had always prayed that God would send her the right husband. When this husband of her dreams eventually abandoned her, she determined to pray for him and to fight *for him with all her strength. In time, her husband returned to her and reconciled himself with God. Now he is one of the leaders in our compassion ministry. Lily is a great example of perseverance, a lady that can make a difference.*

The Bible says that we will be known by our fruits. Lily is someone whose fruit we could envy. She is a woman who loves to pray. She attends all of our vigils without fail and has developed an incredible relationship with the Lord. Even is she is doing chores, she is worshipping. Her house is always neat and tidy and if I visit her while she is cleaning, she is always praying or worshipping at the same time. I enjoy being in her house because there is always a strong sense of the presence of God.

She and her husband Eduardo have developed a program to bless the indigents in Santa Ana. They go out into the streets looking for people who need help. They take them food, make sure they have adequate shelter, and talk to them about the Bible. Sometimes their daughters go along with them. It is wonderful to see the whole family serving the Lord together.

Lily has always been a blessing to me ever since I was little. Now, God uses her in a supernatural way and she continues to be a blessing. Lily has been given a very special gift from God...the gift of prophecy. I consider her to be "the prophet" of our church. Everything that she has prophesied has come to pass in God's timing. I know that many of the good things that I am to receive from the hand of the Lord will in some measure be due to her.

Pastor Melvin Vásquez

An Interview with Liliana

If a man's gift is prophesying, let him use it

in proportion to his faith.

Romans 12:6b

My name is Marta Liliana Vásquez de Yaq but I go by Liliana, or just Lily. I have several things I would like to share with you. First of all, the prophetic gifting that you asked me about actually began when I was an adolescent of fourteen. I never really sought this gift. I just started knowing about things in the church before they occurred. Once I realized what was happening, I felt inadequate because I had only ever heard of adults prophesying. So, basically, I hid the gift.

I learned to consult the Lord in secret. I had a little tape recorder in my room and when the Lord gave me messages,

I would speak in tongues into the recorder. Then, I would be given the interpretation.

A friend of mine, another student, took me to a "prophetic" church. I liked it a lot and started attending there. I was very happy in this little church and I learned a lot and grew spiritually. But, even though it was a "safe" environment for prophecy, I still hid the gift and kept silent, to the point that when I was in my fifteenth year, the gift lay dormant.

About three years passed and I got married. But then, about three years into the marriage, we started having problems. The one good thing is that it woke up my prophetic gift once more. But, many of the things I saw were very sad and it caused me much pain. In addition, I felt really empty inside because of the problems at home with my husband. I used to pray, "God, let my husband see me as a blessing in his life".

I thought the problem would be resolved quickly, but it lasted a long time. My husband even left me for a while.

Perhaps part of it was my own attitude. I was not following the Lord in the way that I knew I should. I got angry very quickly and I harboured things in my heart. Bad words would escape from my mouth. I had no interest in other people. Even when my husband moved back home, things weren't always great.

There was a pause as Lily reflected on some of these things that she had shared.

Author's Question: Lily, can you tell us exactly how you hear from the Lord?

Lily was a little uncomfortable answering. She replied, "I mostly see and I sometimes hear, but I don't like to say anything until I am sure."

Lily continues:

My eldest daughter (also called Lily), was about three years old at this time. Then, I found I was pregnant with my second child, a son. Tragedy struck, and this little boy died before he was born. When I lost the baby, I just cried out in anguish to the Lord. Things got worse between my husband and me. It got to the point where I didn't even want to live in the same house as my husband any more. At this time, God showed me a picture of a door, but it wasn't a door to leave by, it was the door to peace and salvation. I had to make a choice to go through this door. But in reality, I knew it was the only solution. I couldn't go on the way things were. So, I went through that door and it was like I was converted to Jesus all over again! Peace and joy flooded my soul.

It was at this point that one day, an older lady neighbour called me and asked me to come over and pray for her because she had some bad ulcers. I went over and when I saw her legs I said, "Ah, mamasita, these are very painful looking ulcers."

We prayed there and then, and I returned the next afternoon to continue praying for healing.

At that time, there was a program on the television every morning and evening with a preacher that prayed in faith for healings. My neighbour and I liked to watch it. I suddenly went up to the television screen, put my hands on it and said, "Lord, what that man has, I want it too!"

When I returned to my friend's house to pray the next day, she noticed that my attitude had changed. My character had changed too and I didn't act like the same person. God had done a work in me. This whole experience gave me a great victory.

My friend had continued to pray faithfully for herself, but she had also been praying for me. I told her, "I don't have much experience in healing, or much power." Neither did my friend because she was just recently converted. But we resolved to keep praying and believing. Finally the Lord healed her. It turned out that she had diabetes and that this was the cause of her ulcers, but the Lord healed her of the diabetes too.

That boosted my faith and I declared that I was going to shout aloud to the four winds, not just with my voice, but with my hands! These hands were going to be used by the Lord for healing!

Well, moving on, about one year after the death of my son, I found that I was pregnant again with my second daughter Janet. My husband was ecstatic and he started to pray earnestly for the safety of this child. But secretly I was filled with sadness because I had been given a prophetic word. When I was just three months pregnant, a lady came to my house with my mother and she said to me, "Cry out to the Lord for this child. At seven months, this baby is going to have the cord wrapped around its neck three times and will fight for its life." Everything that she said came true to the letter.

Meanwhile, I started praying harder for the daughter in my womb. The Lord spoke to me and told me to prepare myself for a battle in the seventh month because Satan would seek to abort this baby. And so, a strong spiritual battle began!

I declared out loud that my daughter would be a servant of the Most High God, that she would be a preacher of the word and that she would serve the Lord. I continued to pray until the Lord gave me the assurance that the child would be born normal and healthy. Then, when the seventh month came, the prophetic warning came to pass. I had to go the hospital and they performed several examinations. The doctor detected a problem with the baby's heart and he said it was urgent that they bring on the birth of the child. IBut the ultrasound showed that she was only three and a half pounds and that the cord was wrapped three times around her neck. I told the doctor he was crazy if he thought that I would permit him to bring on the birth. I told him that no one was going to touch my daughter, that the Lord had assured me that the baby would be born normal and healthy, and that we would wait. So, I got up and got dressed and left the hospital. When

I got home, my husband asked me how things had gone, and I just said that everything was good.

The pregnancy continued on into my ninth month and the baby managed to get unwrapped from the cord. However, labour did not come and the pregnancy continued into the forty-second week. The doctor said that if the baby did not come in the next couple of days, he was going to do a Caesarean section because the baby would surely die in the womb. I reminded him of what the Lord had said and that he was therefore wrong. This baby would come on its own and would be born without problems! I had another ultrasound and it showed that the baby had stopped growing and that she still weighed only three and one half pounds. The doctor was worried but he wanted to see this pregnancy through to the end because it was his first high risk pregnancy.

I went home and prayed all night. I rubbed anointed oil on my belly. The next day, I prayed and prayed in tongues the whole day. Then, I felt the presence of God enveloping me.

Soon, the contractions started. When they became stronger, I walked to the hospital. All the specialists and a Christian nurse were there and I was the only one giving birth, so I had lots of attention.

When it was almost time for the baby to come, I had an amazing experience. For the very first time, I saw two angels. One stood on either side of me. I gave thanks to the Lord and I started weeping because it was so awesome and something that I didn't really understand. But one angel put a finger to his lips and went "Shhhhh." I took a deep breath and was able to just relax.

When the baby was being born, I felt absolutely no pain. The ultrasound the day before had shown that the baby weighed only three and one half pounds and was very small. When the nurse weighed her, she was ten and one half pounds and fifty-two centimetres long! The cardiologist examined her right away and declared that her heart was perfectly normal. Whatever problem she had before was now gone. She was healthy, just like the Lord had said!

My daughter Janet is now fourteen years old and has always been perfectly healthy. Praise the Lord! I could tell you many more stories but this is the one I would like you to put in your book.

Lily de Yaq

ANGELS AND REVELATIONS

As a young person, my wife Dina was in effect abandoned. Her dad died when she was very young and since her mom couldn't afford to support her, she was given to an aunt to be raised. Thankfully her aunt raised her to know God.

We met when Dina was twelve and I was thirteen. Our relationship as boyfriend and girlfriend was an on-again, off-again affair for several years. Finally, when I was twenty, I proposed and Dina accepted. We got married and lived with my mother for several years. Dina was happy that I was a businessman because she flatly declared she would not marry a pastor. God must have smiled over that one! But, now that she is a pastor's wife, she has accepted the role with joy and enthusiasm. She is the Lord's helpmate chosen specifically for me. Our families were originally not in favour of our marriage because they said it would never last. But this year we just celebrated our twenty-first anniversary!

Dina's trust in God brought us through difficult times. When I walked away from the Lord, she remained faithful and kept on praying for me. Even when we lost a baby boy in pregnancy, Dina's faith never faltered. Later, God gave us our little Emanuel after having first blessed us with three daughters.

Something that I love about Dina is that she is always cheerful. She always has a smile. Dina is a blessing to me and to the church. I would certainly not be who I am today without her.

Pastor Melvin Vásquez

Last night an angel of the God whose I am and whom I

serve stood beside me.

Acts 27:23

DINA

I am Dina de Vásquez, the wife of Pastor Melvin. I have seen angels only one time but it was a huge blessing. It happened only about 1 ½ months ago (that would be April, 2008). It was a Sunday night and there were four of us leading worship at the church. The worship time was very special. Everyone entered in. Suddenly, at the back of the church I saw two angels standing there moving their very large wings. It looked like the wings had feathers but a light shone from them and they were bright and silvery. I really didn't see their faces very well. Their wings moved as if they were fanning the people who were worshipping. It was very hot in the church and this was like a fresh breeze. I would say the angels were about three metres high...very tall.

It was a huge blessing. I couldn't keep singing and just had to put my hands over my face. I started crying with joy. When I opened my eyes and looked up, I couldn't see them any more. At first, I questioned myself and thought, maybe it was my imagination. But I realized that no, they were very real, and it was because of the presence of God. It was a very special service and at this meeting several people got healed. Another interesting thing is that at the same time as the angels, there was the scent of flowers in the air. It was a very beautiful perfume.

I have heard that lots of people in the church have seen angels, but this was the first time I had ever seen them. I feel so privileged that the Lord allowed me to see them even although it was only for a few seconds.

LILY

I remember being in a Wednesday night normal worship service when the ambience suddenly changed while Melvin was preaching. I asked the Lord what was happening. It felt like someone had just turned on air conditioning (although we don't even have fans in the church). It was very fresh.

Suddenly I saw two angels, one on Melvin's right hand side and the other on his left. These angels were tall but not what I would call robust. They were dressed in white garments with gold embroidery. Their eyes were very distinct and it was as if their faces reflected the glory of God. One angel held a vial of oil and was walking back and forth. The other put what I think was honey, on Melvin's lips. His small vial, like the vial of the other angel, was golden in colour. Then the angel with oil poured some on Melvin's head.

The angel with the oil looked at me and I started to cry. I bowed my head and prayed, "Thank you Lord for letting me see this."

Author's Note:

When I asked Melvin about that night, here's what he said.

"I had prepared a message but soon felt that something strange was happening. It seemed like I just talked and talked and talked. It wasn't what I had planned to say. It was like the Holy Spirit just took over. I noticed my sister while I was talking. She seemed to be blinking and staring, and then she bowed her head and was crying. I thought that I must be preaching a terrific message and that it was having a profound effect on her.

There was complete silence in the church. Everybody seemed to stop moving and they were all totally fixed on the message I was giving. I have to admit I was enjoying the whole thing. It wasn't until later though, when I talked with Lily that I realized that she was not in awe of my preaching, but that she was overcome by seeing the angels! I didn't know the angels were there but I did sense that something very special was happening. There was a strong anointing on the ministry time afterwards and lots of people ended up on the floor under the power of God.

Lily continued: Frequently, when the anointing of God is strong in the church, I can see angels at the doors, one on each side. I have actually seen angels several times and I have classified them into three types.

The angels at the doors are warrior angels, tall and robust, and they have large wings. The best way of describing how they appear is that they are dressed a bit like Roman soldiers. They have a white undergarment tunic but they wear a breastplate over it and a wide belt. They wear very beautiful boots. They also have a thin quiver full of arrows and they have a bow.

The angels I have seen at the vigils are of two other types. One group is very robust. They are ministering angels, circulating in and out among the people as they worship. They are all dressed in white. As they move around, they seem attracted to some people but repelled by others. The people they are attracted to seem to be wearing clothes that appear very clean, like new. The people they are repelled by seem to be wearing dirty clothing. Sometimes these people with dirty clothing appear to be worshipping God. They are jumping up and down and clapping to the music. But, it's only on the outside. They are not worshipping with their hearts. Emotion is not necessarily edification. I see this problem frequently with some of the young people.

It's like God is saying that there are some people in the church who are genuinely worshiping Him and pleasing Him but there are others who are harbouring sin. When we come to church, we need to worship God with our whole heart. It doesn't matter if we have problems. We need to put those problems down and worship Him. We need to come asking Him what He would like us to do. We don't just come and say, "Jesus loves me, Jesus loves me". We come willing to be changed. God wants to see fruit.

Well, back to these ministering angels. They have small vials that release wonderful odours. Sometimes it smells like baby powder, sometimes like jasmine. The oil has a smell too. It is a wonderful smell...very rich. The ministering angels circulate and seem to organize the people into groups. Some need to be guided to the front to draw closer to God at the altar. Some need to move aside for healing. Another group is guided to an area to receive the unction of the Holy Spirit and they will fall to the floor. When someone is willing to receive whatever they need from God, the angels pass up and down many times, guiding and leading. But, they don't really touch the people. This is when the air is perfumed.

The third group of angels are also ministering angels. They are smaller in size and very distinct. They actually touch people and appear to be giving hugs. Sometimes I have seen more angels than people in the church. The ministering angels stay a long time in the service. That's about all I can say about angels. I don't really understand it all but I have witnessed that they exist.

NELSON VASQUEZ

Nelson Vásquez is not related to Pastor Melvin although they have the same surname.

I am the co-pastor in Más Que Vencedores church and I try to fulfill my duties in the best ways I possibly can. I used to be active serving in another church, but doors were closing there and new doors were opening to work with Melvin Vásquez, so I joined there and have been with Melvin since the beginning.

One of the strongest supernatural things that happened to me was when I had a vision about three months ago in the church. It was a Monday night prayer night and I was standing off to the side near the doorway to the gym area. The worship team was on the smaller platform at the front, not the big platform up above. The people were enjoying the time of worship because God's presence was very sweet. It was a very special, holy time. Suddenly, I saw a column of fire that rose up from the altar at the front. The best way that I can describe it is that it was like a long passageway or column of fire that extended right up through the roof to the heavenlies. The fire didn't divide or anything, like it did in the Book of Acts. It was more like what Moses and the Israelites must have seen in the desert, I think.

José Vásquez was on the small platform with the worship team and he suddenly dropped the microphone. He described something similar to what I saw. He saw what appeared to be a hole in the roof and a column of fire stretched from the altar upwards. He can confirm what I saw because it was the same thing.

I have seen angels in the past but not at Más Que Vencedores. However, there was an occasion when I knew that angels were present. It was the night that a group of us from the church met to do a prayer walk around the new building. We split up into two groups and marched around the building seven times. When the groups met, we prayed together. As we walked around, we touched the walls with our hands that had been anointed with oil. We declared aloud that God was in this place. I could feel the presence of God get stronger as we marched. There was one moment when I just knew that angels were right there. I could sense their presence. I knew that the angels were possessing the land for the Lord. For a fleeting moment, I thought that I could see something…it was like a reflection and it was white. I tried very hard to see with my physical eyes but I couldn't. However, I knew that there were angels right there because it was the same kind of strong feeling of a presence that I have felt before when I actually did see angels. At the time, I didn't know why God didn't let me see them because I didn't doubt that they were right there. But later, I figured out why. I think we were a little distracted. I remember seeing some young people on the street and it took away my focus. It distracted others and I think it distracted me from what God was going to reveal to me. God is a jealous God. He is very strict about having our whole attention.

But, I have seen angels in the past and I would love to see them again.

Author's question: OK Nelson. Explain to me about another occasion when you have seen angels.

Well, there was the time I went on a retreat. It was at a Catholic Retreat Centre about thirty minutes outside of Santa Ana which was known as a place where you could experience the majesty of God. We stayed there for three days. It consisted of a time of Bible Study, prayer, intercession and ministering. We fasted for the three days. During the retreat, I remember very well our time of intercession. We were part of a group of about twenty-five persons. But, there was one tiny room where you could only enter in twos for about an hour and we took turns. The room had the reputation of having special supernatural things of God take place in it. When it was my turn to go in with a partner, the two young men who were already in there said to us, "Look, we don't want to leave right now because something is happening."

"What's happening?" we asked.

My partner and I entered but the other two lingered. The room is about ten square metres. I was astounded to see that the walls were all covered with oil. We touched the oil and it just kept flowing. It was very sweet-smelling. God allowed us to share in the experience that these two young men were having.

Finally the two youths left, and my partner and I settled down to pray over our intercession list. We prayed for a while then suddenly the ambience changed and we entered spiritual warfare. There was a large black bird about the size of a big eagle that appeared and it circled around us as if it were planning on attacking us. We just prayed fervently for a long time until it left us. When it did go, we could physically feel the presence of God descend.

This room that we were in is very high up and the whole section is shaped like the turret of a castle. There is a part around the top where you can actually walk around. When we left the room and went outside, the two youths that had been in the room before us, were still there and there were two others with them. We stood and watched. One of the youths, who was only about fifteen or sixteen years old, was dancing and laughing and having a great time. The others joined him in a circle and soon they all were dancing. The two men with the young people were dressed in white and sometimes they flew around from one side to the other. They had huge wings that spread out larger than their body. All four of them were worshipping and filled with an extreme joy. It was an awesome sight to see these two young men dancing with angels! I will never forget it.

MELVIN

Author: "*Melvin, have you ever been to this Retreat Centre?*"

Yes I have. On one occasion my brother was working there for two weeks as a volunteer and I went to pick him up to bring him home. It was about ten o'clock in the evening. When I arrived, my brother introduced me to the lady who was in charge at that time. This lady said to me, "Come in, there is something in here for you."

She took my hand and led me to an area near the dining room. I remember she put her hand on me and instantly everything disappeared. All around me everything was white. There was nothing else. And, I started to talk with God! We had a conversation. For me, it was a very short conversation. God told me how much He loved me and that He had big plans for me. He was going to give me a leadership, a work with young people. He was preparing a piece of land for me to work with these young people. At that time, I was a member of a different church. For me, it was a prophetic word. It seemed to be very brief and quick. Then, boom, I was back in the room near the dining area, lying on the floor. The surprise was that people told me I had been talking and laughing and that I had been on the floor for two hours. It was now midnight. I was bathed in sweat and people said that I looked like I had been enjoying the presence of God for two hours although it seemed more like two minutes to me. I have learned that time does not exist for God. For Him, it is the eternal present.

LILY'S PROPHECIES

By Pastor Melvin Vásquez

It was he who gave some to be apostles, some to be

prophets, some to be evangelists, and some to be pastors

and teachers, to prepare God's people for works of

service, so that the body of Christ may be built up.

Ephesians 4:11-12

For several years I worked for the Toyota company in Santa Ana. On one occasion, I was having difficulties in my work and so I spent a lot of time praying with my sister Lily. During the prayer time, she received a word from

243

the Lord and said to me, "Don't worry about your work. The Lord is going to bring you seven potential clients and this will satisfy your bosses and make everything calm for the next year at your job."

Then she added, "God is also going to reward you for your work with the young people. Prepare yourself because you are going to travel outside of the country."

So, I started thanking God for the seven potential clients who would also be the most interesting of clients, and for this upcoming trip. That year, seven new potential clients came! As for the trip, I had always dreamed of going to the United States, so I was thinking that is where I would be going. Some time passed, and then my sister gave me a drawing. She said that she had been praying and the Lord gave her this picture and told her to draw it. It was a map of Central America and South America. I thought, "Wow, South America!"

Well, at that time I was corresponding with a missionary friend over the internet and he said to me, "I have been working with teenagers, but I don't have any program for younger kids". He lives in Argentina.

I said, "Look, I have this great program called Kids' Games." I started sending him manuals. This got me more enthused too, so I started studying more and more about Kids' Games and everything I found, I sent on to my friend. He was thrilled with all the information. Then, before I knew it, I was invited to Argentina, and within fifteen days I was in South America! I praised the Lord, but He wasn't done yet. I received another word that said, "Prepare yourself because you are going to travel a lot more."

The year 2007 was my last year at my work (my secular job). My salary had actually stopped but I was still having to work part time to receive my voucher (money that the company owed to me). This meant I was working less and less hours for a steadily diminishing amount of money until it reached zero. But, it also meant that I was able to commit more and more time to the church and to the Sports' Ministry. And, although I kept earning less and less money this was the time I traveled to ten different countries...Thailand, Japan, Peru, the United States, Costa Rica, Honduras, Nicaragua...and a couple of others. My trip to Thailand for the International Coalition Sports' Congress cost $5500 but I only had to raise $100 of it! It's amazing what you can do with a little money and a lot of faith!

There was another small prophecy from Lily that nevertheless was important to us. When we first moved into our present building, I ordered a hundred chairs although I didn't know how we were going to pay for them. Then Lily gave us a word from the Lord that we should order two hundred chairs.

"Wow," I thought. "How will we pay for all of those chairs?" Well, we decided to believe God and ordered two hundred chairs. It's a good thing too, because now we have way more than one hundred people coming to church. The total bill came to $1,050 and I paid it all at the end of the month in cash. I don't know where the money all came from. Donations just kept coming in and by the end of the month, we had enough! And I'm happy that we have enough chairs for more people. I was going to say that we have two hundred, but actually we have one hundred and ninety-nine because of a "flying incident" when one chair got broken! One of the young men in our congregation had been deep in prayer during one of our vigils. Towards the close of the evening, while everyone was quietly praising God or praying silently, I casually went up to the young man and laid hands on him. He immediately shot backwards, flying through the air, crashing down on a chair, toppling over in a somersault and landing in a sitting position. It was as if he had been struck by an electric bolt! The chair legs collapsed in four directions and we have kept them as a reminder of the power of God.

Question: "Melvin, what is a prophecy that you have received from Lily that you are still waiting to see realized?"

Wow! One of the most precious prophecies I am waiting to see come to pass is regarding your invitation for me to come to Canada to give my testimony. I felt a lot of weight on my shoulders over this because I was to go there and talk about the glory of God and the miracles. And I thought, "What will happen if the anointing doesn't come?"

But at that time, while I was in the church, my sister Lily came to me. I had not said anything to her about my concerns.

She said, "Don't worry. You are very worried but the Lord says, "My glory will descend on your hands. And prepare yourself, because you are going to see the blind receive their sight!"

A couple of nights later, the night I was praying with Samuel and Omar, (Samuel is one of PAN Missions' translators), the Lord spoke again and said, "You are going to see blind eyes being healed". This is something I will see with my very own eyes!

He also said that there would be creative miracles where missing arms would suddenly grow. This is something I don't really understand. It is very powerful. I don't know when this will happen. It would be wonderful to see it happen in Canada, but I really don't know about the timing of this prophecy.

Question: Thanks Melvin. Are there any more prophecies from Liliana that you'd like to share?

There was another prophecy three or four years ago when my sister said that we would have another child, that it would be a boy, and that his name would be Emanuel. We had actually decided that after three girls we did not want any more children. My wife had made the decision to have surgery to prevent conception. But she cancelled it after the prophecy. Then, other women in the church started coming to my wife independently and saying things like, "You are going to have a baby boy in your womb" and "Thanks be to God for the baby boy in your womb." This was long before Dina got pregnant.

Then, two years later, she found out she was going to have a baby. After the ultrasound I asked excitedly, "Well, what is it?"

"It's a boy" the technician said. And when he was born, we named him Emanuel. By the way, my wife has since had the surgery!

Note: Emanuel is now 4 years old.

GOD LOOKS AFTER US

By Pastor Melvin Vásquez

The Lord will watch over your coming and going both

now and forevermore.

Psalm 121: 8

One Thursday night, I remember there was a women's meeting going on at the church. I was there too, along with my brother José. I suddenly felt uncomfortable as if something strange was happening and so I went to the front door. The street was nearly deserted as it usually is in the evenings. It was deserted that is, except for a pair of young guys standing at the front of the church. One of them was Francisco, the leader of this sector of the city, a young homosexual whose pick-up point was right at the main doors. As I stood there, Francisco began urinating as if no one was there in a brazen expression "to mark his territory". He then circled around me and I said to him, "Could you please choose a better please to relieve yourself?"

He looked at me and said, "I can do whatever I want to on this street and furthermore, it's none of your business!"

I then circled around him and replied in a cool tone, "Tonight, only women are attending the church. You could behave more civilized."

He smiled at my words and said, "That doesn't interest me. Period." Then he continued to pour out a barrage of insults.

Finally I said to him, "The only thing I'm going to ask of you is that you be respectful."

At that, he circled around me again, pulling a switch-blade from his pants and waved it close to me saying, "How would you like to have a taste of this? Or would you prefer to back off and shut your mouth?"

Just then, my brother José, who is a lawyer, came to the door and pulled me inside. He immediately took out his cell phone and started dialling his contacts because he wanted to press charges against Francisco. But there was something that didn't sit right with me. I felt that after whatever would happen with Francisco and the police, there would be dire consequences for us later. I left my brother talking on the tele-phone and I started to pray, "Lord, you always do everything perfectly. I believe that calling the police is not the best thing. Lord, what should we do? Can you do something for us?"

I went out the front door and saw that Francisco was no longer there but was now sitting on the curb at the corner of the block. I suddenly felt an impulse to go towards him. It was an urging that overcame my fear...a power greater within me that spurred me on. I did not doubt that God was going to do something in that moment and that He was taking me by the hand closer to Francisco.

When I arrived in front of Francisco I asked, "Can I sit down beside you?"

He replied in the affirmative. I was a little nervous and in my mind I was thinking, "OK Lord, now what do I do?"

My eyes were watching his hands, remembering the switchblade, when suddenly Francisco said to me, "Do you know something? I feel pretty bad. I didn't behave well with you, nor the church, nor with God. Would you forgive me?"

I was astounded and felt like a huge weight had just suddenly been lifted from my heart. This was the beginning of a long conversation with Francisco in which he explained that his mother, an elderly lady who was a Christian, had been praying fervently for him for years and told him many times that God had a purpose for his life. Then for several minutes, our conversation was about the pain of being a prisoner to an affliction such as homosexuality, a lifestyle from which he wanted to escape but that he felt he just couldn't.

I prayed with him, we shook hands, and I invited him to come to one of our services. But he declined saying that everyone would recognize him as "the homosexual" and he would feel uncomfortable.

"But do you know something?" he said with a smile. "I like it when you leave the doors open because I listen to your messages. God touches my heart with the words that come out of your mouth. And when you are singing the choruses, I'm singing along with you. Maybe one day I can change."

The evening was advancing and he said he had to go, that his clients would be coming soon. "But can I offer you something?" he asked.

"Whatever you want" I replied.

"I don't want you to worry about the vehicles of the brothers in the church that get parked on the street" he said. "I will guarantee protection in this place."

Our vehicles had been broken into several times and nobody had ever offered this kind of help. But God was thinking of us and didn't want us worrying about this any more. To this day, Francisco is taking care of us.

When I returned to the church, my brother was complaining that the police had not yet arrived! I explained that God had said, "Wait. I am going to touch a life tonight." That life was Francisco's. And I told him what had happened.

Even though Francisco is not yet attending the church, he still walks up and down the street singing and listening to God's word. One day, God will bring him to the altar. We are waiting for that day.

PARTING WORDS FROM PASTOR MELVIN

Trust in the Lord with all your heart
and lean not on your own understanding;
in all your ways acknowledge Him and He will
make your paths straight.
Proverbs 3:5-6

God moves in all that you permit Him to do in your life.

To walk holding hands with God is the most special thing that a human being can achieve, and the best of all is that He moves in all that we do when we permit Him to totally take control of our lives. We will see great miracles and we will be

257

able to say, "The hand of God is with me." But allow me to tell you that He is really in everything, both big and small.

I was preparing to go to Guatemala City to solicit a visa from the Canadian Embassy there to be able to visit Canada, and the day that I decided to take the bus, I left in the wee, small hours of the morning, travelling to a new place with only an address on a small piece of paper. I arrived in Guatemala City at nine in the morning knowing that the embassy closed their doors to visitors at 11:00a.m., leaving me just two hours to find the Embassy and conduct my business. But something had happened to me on the journey. My relationship with the Lord during the bus ride was very special and I was reluctant to reach my destination and spoil the conversation I was having with the Holy Spirit. I felt as if His arms were hugging me and my heart melted as I felt His touch in my very soul. It was something supernatural.

Suddenly we arrived in Guatemala City and I said to the person sitting beside me that I was going to Zone 10, Street

13, that I was looking for the Canadian Embassy and that I had an appointment at 11:00a.m. This person advised me to get off the bus and take a taxi if I wanted to get there on time. I was mulling it over when a couple of minutes later this person said, "You'd better get off the bus right now".

So, I got off the bus, moved over to one side of the sidewalk and prayed, "Lord, guide me. I'm afraid I'll get lost."

When I raised my head to see where I should go, a building was right in front of me with a lovely red and white flag waving beside it. Letters on the building read "Canadian Embassy". I couldn't believe it. God had let me get off the bus at exactly the right spot. It might be that you would consider this event to be insignificant, but I said to the Lord, "Thank you Holy Spirit for bringing me right here, you have just embraced me one more time with your awesome presence."

After asking for and obtaining my visa, there was nothing left to do but to enter the elevator and fall to my knees, giving thanks to God one more time. On my return to El Salvador on the bus, God was with me again, embracing me and filling me with His Holy Spirit. I arrived home feeling that I could not contain His presence. This day had been one of the best days of my life. God's hand had not been present in a big healing miracle, but I had seen His hand guiding my steps to the right place. He can do this for you too. Allow Him to lead you and He will take you where you need to go.

You might be saying that you have troubles and difficulties in your life. Some things might appear small and insignificant to others but to you they are important. God wants to guide you to the answer. He is your answer! Only call on Him, and allow His hands to guide you. When His hands are upon you, you will never need to worry or fret. Just yield to Him and let Him be your guide.

Amen.

A FINAL WORD

Now it is required that those who have been given a trust

must prove faithful.

I Cor. 4:2

I f we keep adding stories of God's miracles, this book will never go to print. But, I'm going to close with a little story about my daughter Katrin. This happened just recently. Katrin turned fourteen a little while ago and is becoming aware of who she is. Like a typical fourteen year old girl, she is concerned about her appearance. I think she has a beautiful face with lovely eyes. I also think she has a charming smile, but for her, her smile was an embarrassment. She has always been missing a tooth in the front of her mouth. It was never an issue until she started getting teased about it at school. It got to the point where she tried not to smile and was constantly putting her hand up to her face to hide the gap.

Finally Katrin came to me crying. She was suffering psychologically and was feeling downright miserable. She wanted a miracle. I invited her to pray with me at 3:00a.m. to ask God for a tooth. She jumped at the chance. I told her that we would pray for exactly one week then believe God for the miracle. The first night I went to her bedroom door at 3:00a.m., knocked softly and called her name. She came out immediately because she had been sitting on the edge of the bed eagerly awaiting the time.

We passed a week praying together. For me, it was a very special time to pray with my daughter as she cried out to God with her Dad at her side. At the end of the week, during our 3:00a.m. prayer time, Katrin cried out, "Dad, I feel something".

I examined her mouth and saw the tell-tale white of a new tooth pushing through her gum. Today, that tooth is just about fully grown. When our children suffer, we can use the situation as the perfect time to teach them how to reach out to God. It is a wonderful opportunity for them to learn how to pray in faith and to show them that God really cares and that He has the answer to everything in life.

God bless each one of you. Thank you for letting me share about what God is doing in our life, in my family, in our church. May your life be blessed abundantly!

Pastor Melvin Vásquez

After re-reading all the stories and re-living all the wonderful visits we had made with some very special people, the uppermost question in our minds is of course, why don't we have miracles happening in our church like they do in Más Que Vencedores? Why haven't we experienced angelic visitations and supernatural occurrences? Our church is evangelical, sound in doctrine, Bible believing, mission-minded and outward reaching. We have a great pastor who preaches the Word, faithful prayer warriors, great music and lots of good programs. We have earnestly sought revival and seek to yield ourselves to God's will. We remember some healings that have taken place in the past, but nothing near the scale of what is going on in Pastor Melvin's church.

It seems too trite and too easy to say that El Salvador, as part of Latin America, is a relatively poor nation and that God seems to manifest Himself more in these poor nations. If that is so, as we have often heard spoken, then it still begs the question, "Why?"

We don't profess to have all the answers but we do have some observations. We have discovered that the Pastor and probably all of those who were interviewed have given over their lives to the Lord in the strictest sense of the words. They bring God into their conversations, talk to Him all day, and worship Him with abandon. They sacrifice of their time and resources willingly and steadily. Their walk with God is not a nicely slotted piece of their lives. It is their raison d'être, their whole life's purpose. They fast regularly, intercede for others faithfully (many at 3:00a.m.), give to others poorer than themselves (and most are quite poor) and attend worship services and vigils where they participate with mind, body and spirit. When interviewed, Nelson Vásquez said at one point, that God is a jealous God. We recognize the truth of that and have come to believe that God expects this 100% kind of devotion from His children. When we do that, He is pleased. When the whole church does that, He moves. The late Smith Wigglesworth, who saw countless miracles of God occur in the early 20th century, said, "To be filled with the Spirit we must yield and submit, until our bodies are saturated with God, that at any moment God's will can be revealed." We believe that many in Pastor Melvin's church, including Melvin himself, are "yielded" to God and "saturated" with the Holy Spirit.

As Melvin preaches and shares his stories to believers in Canada, it is our hope that churches will be re-energized and challenged to follow God with unwavering devotion and to consciously bring Him into every aspect of our lives. In other words, to do what we know we should do but from which we get distracted so easily. As Melvin says, and we believe it, God is more than willing to manifest Himself to us. But it would seem that we have to do our part.

Now to him who is able to do immeasurably more

than all we ask or imagine,

according to his power that is at work within us,

to him be the glory in the church

and in Christ Jesus throughout all generations,

for ever and ever! Amen.

Ephesians 3:20-21

Blessings,

Annette Vickers

and

Deb Coutts

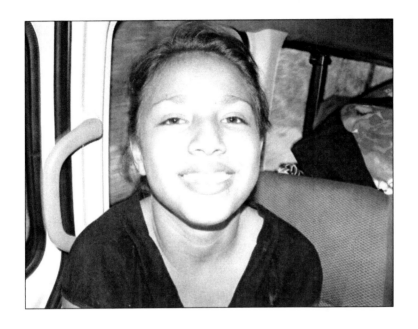

We want to leave you with this image of Pastor Melvin's daughter, Katrin, proudly showing the new tooth that God gave her (the slightly smaller tooth in the front). What a beautiful way to remember that our heavenly father loves us and cares for us.

LaVergne, TN USA
10 September 2009
157520LV00001B/27/P